Hesse Place Name Indexes:
Identifying Place Names
Using Alphabetical and
Reverse Alphabetical Indexes

Roger P. Minert, Ph.D., A.G.

GRT Publications

Publisher's Cataloging in Publication

Minert, Roger P.

  Hesse Place Name Indexes/ by Roger P. Minert

        p. cm.

ISBN: 0-9678420-0-X
Library of Congress Catalog Card Number: 00-130124

Second Printing, 2000.

GRT Publications, Woods Cross, Utah

Table of Contents

The castle and village of Munzenberg.

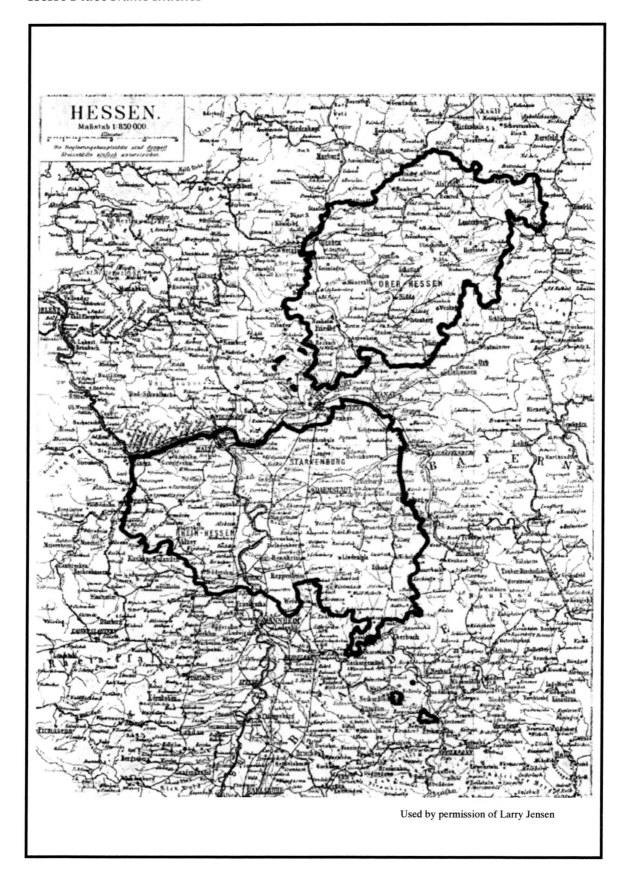

Used by permission of Larry Jensen

Introduction

Over the last few centuries the name *Hessen* has been used in connection with numerous major and minor regions of West Central Germany and as such represents a potential source of confusion. This is especially true for family history researchers attempting to identify the locations of ancestral homes. Besides the large political entities of the Grand Duchy of Hesse *(Großherzogtum Hessen,* often referred to as *Hessen-Darmstadt)* and the Prussian province of *Hessen-Nassau,* there are smaller regions such as *Rheinhessen, Oberhessen,* and *Hessen-Starkenburg* (in the Grand Duchy) and *Hessen-Kassel* and *Kurhessen-Waldeck* (in *Hessen-Nassau*).

This index includes the names of all identifiable places in the Grand Duchy of Hesse *(Großherzogtum Hessen).* As shown on the map opposite, the Grand Duchy consisted essentially of two large regions separated by a narrow section of *Hessen-Nassau* with the city of *Frankfurt am Main.* The northern region was generally called *Oberhessen* and the southern *Hessen-Starkenburg* or simply *Starkenburg,* and included *Rheinhessen* to the west. A half-dozen tiny exclaves are scattered to the west of *Frankfurt am Main* and to the south of *Starkenburg.*

Portions of Hesse as a political entity date back to the 14th century, while others were annexed quite recently, such as *Rheinhessen* to the west of *Starkenburg* in 1815. The map represents the greatest extent of the Grand Duchy as it existed from 1871 to 1945. The places listed in this index can be found within that territory.

The names of places found in this index were taken from two sources:

> *Amtliches Verzeichnis der Gemeinden in Hessen, Volkszählung 1950* [Official Index of the Towns in Hesse--Census of 1950]. [Family History Library book no. 943.41 E5a]
>
> *Kirchenbücher und Standesregister für alle Wohnplätze im Land Hessen* [Church and Civil Records for All Locations in the Province of Hesse], ed. Otfried Praetorius, Darmstadt, 1939. [Family History Library book no. 943.41 K23p and microfilm no. 492895]

Today the borders of Hesse are again quite different. Formed officially in 1949, the Federal *Bundesland Hessen* includes practically all of *Oberhessen, Starkenburg, Hessen-Nassau,* and *Hessen-Kassel. Rheinhessen* is now a part of *Rheinland-Pfalz.*

The names of localities in the Prussian provinces of *Hessen-Nassau* and *Waldeck* (*Kurhessen-Waldeck*) can be found in the *Gemeindelexikon für das Königreich Preußen* [Gazetteer for the Kingdom of Prussia], vols. 10 and 11 respectively [FHL book nos. 943 E5kp and microfilm nos. 491042 and 1187921-item 4]. A reverse alphabetical index for *Hessen-Nassau* is in preparation.

I am grateful to Daniel Schlyter, Larry Jensen, and Wolfgang Lebedies -- staff members of the Family History Library in Salt Lake City -- for their advice and assistance in the preparation of this index. Design and illustrations provided by Todd Roach. Cassie Minert helped with data entry.

It is my sincere hope that this reverse alphabetical index will contribute to the faster and more efficient identification of place names. Users should feel free to inform me of any deficiencies or mistakes in this index -- they are mine alone.

Roger P. Minert
Woods Cross, Utah
November 1999

A typical village in *Oberhessen*

How to Use the *Reverse Alphabetical Index*

It is often difficult to decipher names found in church and civil records written in German. When the initial letter is illegible, blotted out, lost in a tight binding, or lost due to torn or moulded pages, an actual deciphering of the name can be impossible. A gazetteer is usually insufficient help when the first few letters of a place name are missing. It also happens on occasion that a researcher will (despite his best efforts) inaccurately extract a place name that is intact, and then be unable to locate the place on a map.

The reverse alphabetical index is designed for use in situations such as these. It allows the researcher to work from the end of the place name toward the beginning to form the correct name, to test a theoretical spelling, or at least to formulate "candidate" names for further investigation.

For example, if only the letters *...gwaden* can be distinguished clearly in a record, one will find in this index (by reading from the final "n" toward the start of the word) that the only town in the *Großherzogtum Hessen* ending with the letters *...gwaden* is *Langwaden*. The researcher can then return to the record in question to determine how well the name *Langwaden* might match the handwritten version.

[page 14]   Klein-Karben
Groß-Karben
Staden
Lan**gwaden**
Kohden
Inheiden
Ofleiden

The same list can be used to test the spelling of a theoretical extraction. For example, if the researcher were to erroneously read *Langwaden* as *Sangwaden* or *Tangwaden*, he could test out the spelling against the index and make the appropriate adjustment.

Of course it is not impossible that the recognizable letters are common to more than one place name. For example, the seven final letters *...zelbach* occur in the names of three different towns: *Wurzelbach, Litzelbach,* and *Lützelbach.*

[page 7]   Kesselbach
Quattelbach
Wur**zelbach**
Lit**zelbach**
Lüt**zelbach**
Zahlbach
Kailbach

If it is still impossible to determine which one of the three is correct, the next step in the identification process would be a search of church or civil records of each parish -- beginning with whichever town is closest to the town in which the original record was compiled.

Another common reason for consulting the reverse alphabetical index is to convert an archaic spelling of a place name into the modern version. For example, the town name *Crumbach* was written *Krumbach* and even *Grumbach* years ago. The name *Beerfelden* is also found in old records as *Bärfelden, Berfelden* and *Behrfelden*. In each case, the names end with the same letters and can be tracked down when one reads from the end of the name toward the beginning.

Because the task facilitated by this reverse alphabetical index is that of ascertaining the proper spelling of specific place names, those names shared by more than one locality are not specifically designated as such in this list. For example, there are no fewer than three towns named *Rohrbach*, but that name occurs only once in this index. The method described above would be employed to identify the *Rohrbach* in question.

In some cases a modifier has been added to a town name over the years to distinguish it from other towns of the same name. An example would be *Jugenheim an der Bergstraße* vs. *Jugenheim in Rheinhessen*, or simply *Jugenheim*. This reverse alphabetical index features *Jugenheim* in three places -- one ending with -*m,* one with -*e,* and one with -*n.*

Once the correct name (or best "candidate") has been chosen, the researcher can refer to the church book inventory mentioned above to learn more about existing vital records. For additional information on the location, the best alternative reference source is *Meyers Orts- und Verkehrslexikon des Deutschen Reichs* [Meyer's Gazetteer and Commercial Directory of the German Empire], published in 1913 [FHL book no. 943 E5mo and microfilm nos. 496640 ff.].

Because it can just as easily happen that the end of a place name is not legible, a regular alphabetical listing of all locations in *Großherzogtum Hessen* is also provided herein.

The reader should bear in mind that the letters *ä, ö,* and *ü* are arranged alphabetically under *a,o,* and *u* -- as if there were no *Umlaut.* The German symbol *ß* (*ss*) is treated as if it were only one *s.*

Gebrauchsanweisung

Es kommt des öfteren vor, daß der Familienforscher die im Kirchenbuch oder Standesamtsregister vorkommenden Orts- und Personennamen nicht lesen oder entziffern kann. Ist der Anfangsbuchstabe nicht leserlich, verblasst, im Faltz versteckt oder gar nicht vorhanden (die Seite ist abgerissen oder zerfranzt), so ist das Entziffern unmöglich. Meistens hilft kein Ortsverzeichnis, wenn beispielsweise die ersten drei oder vier Buchstaben eines Ortsnamens fehlen. Manchmal liest der Forscher einen sichtbaren Ortsnamen falsch ab und findet ihn folglich weder auf der Landkarte noch im Ortsverzeichnis.

Das vorliegende Verzeichnis soll in solchen Fällen als Hilfe dienen, indem es dem Forscher ermöglicht, von hinten nach vorne den Ortsnamen zu ermitteln, bzw. wenigstens mögliche und passende Namen vorzuschlagen, die dann auf die Richtigkeit hin geprüft werden können.

Zum Beispiel, blieben lediglich die Letztbuchstaben des Ortsnamens *...gwaden* im Eintrag leserlich, so fängt man im vorliegenden Verzeichnis beim Lesen des entsprechenden Ortsnamens von hinten an -- also beim *"n"* -- und liest rückwärts auf den Anfang des Namens zu. Dadurch wird ersichtlich, dass der Name eines einzigen Ortes im Großherzogtum Hessen so endet, nämlich *Langwaden.* Mit dieser Erkenntnis wendet sich der Forscher nun wiederum dem in Frage kommenden Eintrag zu und versucht, Theorie und Praxis zu vergleichen, ob der Name nicht doch zu entziffern ist.

[Seite 14]	Klein-Karben
	Groß-Karben
	Staden
	Lang**waden**
	Kohden
	Inheiden
	Ofleiden

Schreibt der Forscher (mit der besten Absicht) den Namen irrtümlich als *Sangwaden* oder *Tangwaden* ab und findet ihn im Ortsverzeichnis daher nicht, so kann der theoretische Ortsname mit ähnlich endenden verglichen und die Korrektur vorgenommen werden.

Es kann natürlich auch vorkommen, dass die letzten leserlichen Buchstaben am Ende eines Namens bei mehr als einem Ortsnamen vorkommen. Beispielsweise gibt es dieselben letzten sieben Buchstaben *...zelbach* in den Namen dreier Ortschaften: *Wurzelbach, Litzelbach,* und *Lützelbach.*

[Seite 7]	Kesselbach
	Quattelbach
	Wur**zelbach**
	Lit**zelbach**
	Lüt**zelbach**
	Zahlbach
	Kailbach

Ist der Forscher nicht in der Lage, unter den drei Ortschaften zu unterscheiden, so setzt man in den Kirchenbüchern oder Standesamtsregistern der drei Ortschaften die Suche fort. Am besten fängt man in dem nächstliegendenen Ort an.

Ein weiterer allgemein üblicher Grund für die Benutzung des *Reverse Alphabetical Index* bestünde darin, einen altertümlich buchstabierten Ortsnamen in seine gegenwärtige Schreibweise zu übertragen. Zum Beispiel war der Name des Ortes *Crumbach* vor Jahren unter *Krumbach* oder sogar *Grumbach* zu finden. Der Ortsname Beerfelden erscheint in alten Urkunden auch unter *Bärfelden, Berfelden* und *Behrfelden.* In jedem Fall endet der Ortsname jedoch mit denselben Buchstaben und ist somit ermittelbar, wenn man ihn im vorliegenden Verzeichnis von hinten nach vorn liest.

Es geht bei diesem alphabetisch rückwärts sortierten Verzeichnis um die Feststellung eines Ortsnamens. Daher ist es an dieser Stelle nicht massgebend, die gleichlautenden Namen der Ortschaften anzugeben. Zum Beispiel kommt der Ortsname *Rohrbach* im Grossherzogtum Hessen dreimal vor, hier in diesem Verzeichnis allerdings nur einmal. Die oben erwähnte Methode kann angewandt werden, damit das richtige *Rohrbach* gefunden wird.

Bei mehreren Ortsnamen gibt es nähere Beschreibungen, weil man sich schon damals dessen bewusst war, dass derselbe Name mehr als einmal verwendet wurde. Es gibt beispielsweise *Jugenheim an der Bergstraße* und *Jugenheim in Rheinhessen.* Im örtlichen Register schrieb man vielleicht nur *Jugenheim,* weil es jedem geläufig war. Im vorliegenden Verzeichnis findet man den Namen *Jugenheim* vorsichtshalber an drei Stellen, in *-n, -e,* und *-m* endend.

Falls zwei oder mehr Ortschaften gleichen Namens als "Kandidaten" aufgeführt sind, wende man sich an das Ortsverzeichnis und das Kirchenbuchverzeichnis, die beide in der *Introduction* (Einführung) des vorliegenden Werkes erwähnt sind, um festzustellen, wo sich weitere Register befinden. Zusätzlich kann man sich des 1913 von Meyer herausgegebenen *Orts- und Verkehrslexikon des Deuschen Reichs* bedienen.

Weil es vorkommen könnte, dass der Forscher das Ende eines Namens nicht entziffern kann, folgt dem alphabetisch rückwärts geordneten Verzeichnis ein normales alphabetisches der Ortsnamen im Großherzogtum Hessen.

Die Leserin/der Leser möchte sich stets vor Augen halten, dass in diesem Verzeichnis die Buchstaben *ä, ö,* und *ü* so eingeordnet sind, als gäbe es keinen Umlaut, desgleichen die entsprechenden großgeschriebenen Buchstaben. Das Zeichen *ß* wird im Folgenden wie ein einzelnes *s* behandelt.

Reverse Alphabetical Index of the Grand Duchy of Hesse

Corsica	Frankenfeld
Nidda	Hüttenfeld
Fauerbach bei Nidda	Wohnfeld
Geiß-Nidda	Crainfeld
Felda	Krainfeld
Klein-Felda	Blofeld
Lumda	Wetterfeld
Klein-Lumda	Fürfeld
Allendorf an der Lumda	Alsfeld
Treis an der Lumda	Hopfmannsfeld
Eifa	Bernsfeld
Ulfa	Büßfeld
Maria	Rixfeld
Korsika	-Hof, Wild
Willina	Semd
Rauna	Eiserne Hand
Hayna	-Hof, Sand
Traisa	Altensand
Ober-Traisa	Kornsand
Nieder-Trausa	Brauerschwend
Rad	Grund
Hofheim im Ried	Fürstengrund
Langd	Haingrund
Wald	Eutergrund
Harbwald	Rebsgrund
-Hof, Wald	Fronkelsgrund
-Hof, Stubenwald	Rapsgrund
Reichelsheim im Odenwald	Sommersgrund
Höchst im Odenwald	Kreutzersgrund
Nauheimer Oberwald	Melchiorsgrund
Treburer Oberwald	Oberod
Niederwald	Annerod
Laubacher Wald	Bannerod
Lorscher Wald	Winnerod
Weilerwald	Engelrod
Treburer Unterwald	Dotzelrod
Kreiswald	Romrod
Allmendfeld	Schwabenrod
Lengfeld	Elbenrod
Schleifeld	Vadenrod

Bleidenrod	Hof, Beunde
Bodenrod	Riedrode
Dudenrod	Burg Gräfenrode
Kefenrod	Herchenrode
Rülfenrod	-Hof, See
Angenrod	Tempelsee
Stangenrod	Ulvenhöfe
Eichenrod	Siegmundshäuser Höfe
Eschenrod	Pfälzer Höfe
Bockenrod	Mönchshöfe
Vockenrod	-Hof, Herberge
Allenrod	Kiliansherberge
Wallenrod	Sorge
Reimenrod	Lache
Allmenrod	Krausebuche
Ermenrod	Saubuche
Dannenrod	Marienhöhe
Elpenrod	Fauerbach vor der Höhe
Appenrod	Rodheim vor der Höhe
Oppenrod	Pfefferhöhe
Hartenrod	Ludwigshöhe
Reibertenrod	Juhöhe
Seibertenrod	Trohe
Ober-Seibertenrod	Utphe
Unter-Seibertenrod	Kuhruhe
Stumpertenrod	Löwenruhe
Ruppertenrod	Albertsruhe
Hattenrod	Fasanerie
Betzenrod	Frauenhecke
Blitzenrod	Höllerhecke
Rainrod	Mücke
Reinrod	Sandwoogbrücke
Göbelnrod	Apfelbachbrücke
Sellnrod	Stollmühle
Nonrod	Kohlwiese
Oberrod	Heppenheim an der Wiese
Bersrod	Steinertswiese
Zeilhard	Holzwiese
Litzard	Hutzwiese
Kohlgrube	Heppenheim an der Bergstraße
Taschengrube	Jugenheim an der Bergstraße
Silbergrube	Grundhause
Kaisergrube	Waldschützenhause
Breitenhaide	Rote Warte
Heide	Nikolauspforte

Hellenhütte	Hilsig-Hof
Emelinenhütte	Vohberg-Hof
Glashütte	Burghof
Thomashütte	Mönchhof
Gebhardshütte	Wildehirschhof
Ludwigshütte	Bruchhof
Kernbachs-Hütte	Lohhof
Friedrichshütte	Tal-Hof
Kortelshütte	Hospital-Hof
Salmshütte	Hospital Hof
Sandaue	Scheibelhof
Alte Sandaue	Angelhof
Lang-Aue	Mangelhof
Blei-Aue	Engelhof
Rückenaue	Hassel-Hof
Nonnen-Aue	Mühl-Hof
Hessenaue	Hell-Hof
Oberaue	Höllhof
Ober-Aue	Bremhof
Fulder Aue	Helm-Hof
Maulbeeraue	Heidenhof
Königsklinger Aue	Weidenhof
Jakobsberger Aue	Linden-Hof
Knoblochsaue	Pfaffenhof
Lebertsaue	Selgen-Hof
Lothary-Aue	Silgen-Hof
Horloff	Fängenhof
Rodheim an der Horloff	Lerchenhof
Trais-Horloff	Amalienhof
Wolf	Marien-Hof
Hof	Plackenhof
Wald-Holf	Heckenhof
Stubenwald-Hof	Hecken-Hof
Wildhof	Kannengießerhechenhof
Wild-Hof	Huckenhof
Sandhof	Falken-Hof
Sand-hof	Finken-Hof
Windhof	Eulenhof
Gundhof	Salinenhof
Mörfelden-Gundhof	Christinenhof
Beunde Hof	Nonnen-Hof
Seehof	Herrenhof
See-Hof	Wiesen-Hof
Herberge-Hof	Plattenhof
Schafhof	Henriettenhof

Löwenhof	Staudenheimer Hof
Layen-Hof	Bockenheimer Hof
Klein-Hof	Bettenheimer Hof
Schelln-Hof	Heyenheimer Hof
Schönhof	Bonnheimer Hof
Fronhof	Bornheimer Hof
Hainaer Hof	Bensheimer Hof
Arnheider Hof	Gommersheimer Hof
Altenfelder Hof	Oberstraßheimer Hof
Sensfelder Hof	Boxheimer Hof
Olfer Hof	Kammerhof
Wolfer-Hof	Sommerhof
Altdörfer Hof	Oberseener Hof
Jäger-Hof	Hainer Hof
Flensunger Hof	Bollhainer Hof
Fengenberger Hof	Petershainer Hof
Kahlenberger Hof	Gehaborner Hof
Wiesberger Hof	Treburer Hof
Vogelsberger Hof	Maltheserhof
Steckelsberger Hof	Breitwieser Hof
Vöckelsberger Hof	Häuser Hof
Albacher Hof	Riedhäuser Hof
Kröckelbacher Hof	Stockhäuser Hof
Erbacher Hof	Retschenhäuser Hof
Laubacher Hof	Hohenhäuserhof
Westphälischer Hof	Mückenhäuser Hof
Preußischer Hof	Wellershäuser Hof
Falkscher Hof	Karthäuser Hof
Geygerscher Hof	Hexthäuser Hof
Rosscher Hof	Darmstädter Hof
Haxenbucher Hof	Wetterhof
Weiherhof	Ritterhof
Grünhecker Hof	Ringauer Hof
Birker Hof	Mayer-Hof
Biedenthaler Hof	Remayer Hof
Rauenthaler Hof	Geyer-Hof
Dorndieler Hof	Beinhards Hof
Weilerhof	Leonhards-Hof
Aechzeller Hof	Tönges-Hof
Krämer-Hof	Dammeshof
Rodheimer Hof	Vietmes-Hof
Bischheimer Hof	Steines-Hof
Münchbischheimer Hof	Grünes-Hof
Schwalheiomer Hof	Schlieglofs-Hof
Wahlheimer Hof	Johannis-Hof

Ziergiebelshof	Borsdorf
Dippelshof	Roßdorf
Bastelshof	Eudorf
Karls-Hof	Neudorf
Stockmannshof	Hutzdorf
Hoppers-Hof	Kirtorf
Geiß-Hof	Wolfslauf
Rückerts-Hof	Diebach am Haag
Hardthof	Herrnhaag
Schardt-Hof	Schönmattenwaag
Richthof	Ober-Schönmattenwaag
Wart-Hof	Unter-Schönmattenwaag
Schmitt-Hof	Gehag
Au-Hof	Metzlos-Gehag
Neuhof	Hasselhag
Pfalzhof	Buchschlag
Kuralpe Kreuzhof	Lempelstieg
Kühkopf	Albig
Altenschlirf	Planig
Walldorf	König
Strebendorf	-Hof, Hilsig
Niedendorf	Kinzig
Sickendorf	Mittel-Kinzig
Ober-Sickendorf	Ober-Kinzig
Unter-Sickendorf	Nieder-Kinzig
Allendorf	Lang
Großendorf	-Aue, Lang
Renzendorf	Bing
Weitzendorf	Mümling
Londorf	Hering
Oberndorf	Claraberg
Niederndorf	Friedberg
Storndorf	Kaffeeberg
Konradsdorf	Rechberg
Ludwigsdorf	Kirchberg
Seibelsdorf	Hohberg
Eichelsdorf	-Hof, Vohberg
Ilsdorf	Eichelberg
Solms-Ilsdorf	Hasselberg
Consdorf	Kohlberg
Hergersdorf	Bamberg
Heckersdorf	Neu-Bamberg
Höckersdorf	Homberg
Wallersdorf	Lindenberg
Eulersdorf	Schiffenberg

Staufenberg

Ziegenberg

Heiligenberg

Zwingenberg

Krähenberg

Reichenberg

Rothenberg

Marienberg

Rockenberg

Lichtenberg

Rodau bei Lichtenberg

Ortenberg

Hüttenberg

Münzenberg

Trais-Münzenberg

Steinberg

Watzenborn-Steinberg

Ober-Steinberg

Schönberg

Dornberg

Grünberg

Bieberberg

Wirberg

Jakobsberg

Geisberg

Johannisberg

Felsberg

Helmsberg

Darsberg

Ebersberg

Kellersberg

Gumpersberg

Lißberg

Wißberg

Brometsberg

Veitsberg

Kochertsberg

Hausen am Hausberg

Rochusberg

Antoniusberg

Glauberg

Heuberg

Breuberg

Burg Breuberg

Laurenzberg

Würzberg

Otzberg

Hotzberg

Sorg

Ober-Sorg

Unter-Sorg

Dianaburg

Dieburg

Ronneburg

Amöneburg

Ganseburg

Hammelburg

Badenburg

Isenburg

Neu-Isenburg

Altenburg

Krötenburg

Ostenburg

Krotzenburg

Klein-Krotzenburg

Oberburg

Wasserburg

Schwabsburg

Friedrichsburg

Arnsburg

Bernsburg

Jägersburg

in der Straßburg

Ruppertsburg

Gustavsburg

Ginsheim-Gustavsburg

Neuburg

Kreuzburg

Sandbach

Diebach

Aulen-Diebach

Unterdiebach

Kunnebach

Minchbach

Aschbach

Eschbach

Ober-Eschbach

Nieder-EschFischbach

Münschbach

Wünschbach

Pfirschbach
Hetschbach
Rehbach
Maibach
Raibach
Pfalzraibach
Albach
Calbach
Raidelbach
Ober-Raidelbach
Unter-Raidelbach
Heidelbach
Mengelbach
Ober-Mengelbach
Unter-Mengelbach
Michelbach
Wald-Michelbach
Kröckelbach
Melbach
Hammelbach
Hesselbach
Kesselbach
Quattelbach
Wurzelbach
Litzelbach
Lützelbach
Zahlbach
Kailbach
Zeilbach
Wallbach
Illbach
Maulbach
Eulbach
Gambach
Hambach
Ober-Hambach
Unter-Hambach
Hembach
Wembach
Himbach
Schimbach
Kimbach
Climbach
Klimbach
Rimbach

Lützel-Rimbach
Galmbach
Holmbach
Kolmbach
Mombach
Rombach
Brombach
Kirch-Brombach
Langen-Brombach
Frau-Rombach
Mumbach
Ober-Mumbach
Nieder-Mumbach
Unter-Mumbach
Crumbach
Fränkisch-Crumbach
Mainzisch-Crumbach
Krumbach
Grubenbach
Ober-Grubenbach
Unter-Grubenbach
Schadenbach
Liedenbach
Nieder-Raidenbach
Breidenbach
Ober-Breidenbach
Nieder-Breidenbach
Unter-Breidenbach
Seidenbach
Rodenbach
Lardenbach
Ober-Laudenbach
Offenbach
Bleichenbach
Reichenbach
Waschenbach
Fleschenbach
Deckenbach
Bickenbach
Flockenbach
Unter-Flockenbach
Finkenbach
Ober-Finkenbach
Unter-Finkenbach
Ellenbach

Klein-Ellenbach	Leberbach
Dürr-Ellenbach	Liederbach
Gras-Ellenbach	Effolderbach
Schöllenbach	Sonderbach
Erlenbach	Beerbach
Wald-Erlenbach	Schmal-Beerbach
Ober-Erlenbach	Ober-Beerbach
Nieder-Erlenbach	Nieder-Beerbach
Airlenbach	Dorf-Erbach
Mörlenbach	Kocherbach
Schannenbach	Bierbach
Linnenbach	Schlierbach
Wippenbach	Stierbach
Fahrenbach	Höllerbach
Ohrenbach	Affhöllerbach
Schnorrenbach	Affolterbach
Eisenbach	Hinterbach
Geisenbach	Haisterbach
Rosenbach	Kelsterbach
Dusenbach	Neu-Kelsterbach
Breitenbach	Otterbach
Rai-Breitenbach	Lauterbach
Klein-Breitenbach	Auerbach
Groß-Breitenbach	Fauerbach
Faustenbach	Friedberg-Fauerbach
Bettenbach	Leuerbach
Hottenbach	Lehrbach
Lanzenbach	Löhrbach
Kunzenbach	Rohrbach
Lörzenbach	Ober-Rohrbach
Dietzenbach	Lorbach
Zotzenbach	Amorbach
Wohnbach	Wald-Amorbach
Hainbach	Wüst-Amorbach
Steinbach	Asbach
Bollnbach	Pferdsbach
Kernbach	Mönchsbach
Hornbach	Alsbach
Harbach	Balsbach
Scharbach	Elsbach
Ober-Scharbach	Wiebelsbach
Unter-Scharbach	Lützel-Wiebelsbach
Marbach	Pfalzwiebelsbach
Erbach	Egelsbach
Eberbach	Igelsbach

Mangelsbach	Kreidach
Vöckelsbach	Ober-Kreidach
Melsbach	Unter-Kreidach
Gammelsbach	Berkach
Hämmelsbach	Steinach
Annelsbach	Absteinach
Hippelsbach	Ober-Absteinach
Kilsbach	Unter-Absteinach
Eulsbach	Neckar-Steinach
Brensbach	Abtsteinach
Sensbach	Urberach
Ober-Sensbach	Eich
Unter-Sensbach	Hain in der Dreieich
Kainsbach	Philippseich
Ober-Kainsbach	Beyerseich
Nieder-kainsbach	Garbenteich
Ernsbach	Kälberteich
Mosbach	Steinbrückerteich
Rosbach	Lich
Ober-Rosbach	Rittschlich
Nieder-Rosbach	Haberich
Liebersbach	Kestrich
Neckar-Liebersbach	Münch
Ober-Liebersbach	im Windloch
Nieder-Liebersbach	Eichloch
Unter-Liebersbach	Heppenheim im Loch
Albersbach	Sörgenloch
Angersbach	Finkenloch
Schleiersbach	Wasserloch
Wächtersbach	Haßloch
Waltersbach	Heßloch
Güttersbach	Lorsch
Gaßbach	Neutsch
Meßbach	Flockenbusch
Roßbach	Oberbusch
Spechtbach	Mittlerer Busch
Streitbach	Seidenbuch
Glattbach	Steinbuch
Stettbach	Erbuch
Laubach	Mönchbruch
Raubach	Gräbenbruch
Heubach	Grafenbruch
Erzbach	auf dem Loh
Hetzbach	Breitenloh
Butzbach	Berngeroth

Reimeroth	Neuthal
Mummenroth	-Hof, Tal
Nonnenroth	-Hof, Hospital
Hassenroth	Hof, Hospital
Hummetroth	Philippshospital
Wörth	Wiesental
Mühlwörth	Schannenbacher Tal
Roggenwörth	Stettbacher Tal
Schusterwörth	Vilbel
Steinswörth	Nübel
Kisselau-Wörth	Griedel
Fürth	Einsiedel
Wegfurth	Maria-Einsiedel
Ober-Wegfurth	Stallenkandel
Unter-Wegfurth	Roter Kandel
Egelfurth	Rendel
Steinfurth	Södel
Beerfurth	Staffel
Kirch-Beerfurth	Bürgel
Pfaffen-Beerfurth	Dorndiel
Bellmuth	Lämmerspiel
Lindenstruth	im Steinbickel
Kuh	Lotzenbuckel
Rai	Zuckerbuckel
Nack	Frankel
Hasselheck	Winkel
Wieseck	Weisel
Philippseck	Hoch-Weisel
Buseck	Nieder-Weisel
Großen-Buseck	Trösel
Alten-Buseck	Hässel
Queck	-Hof, Hassel
Mitteldick	Messel
Neuwerk	Grube Messel
Ziegelschal	Leusel
Engelthal	Münch-Leusel
Tiefenthal	Hengmantel
Offenthal	Kastel
Langenthal	Forstel
Hüttenthal	Lützel
Liebfrauenthal	Hebstahl
Löwenthal	Ober-Hebstahl
Brunnthal	Unter-Hebstahl
Jägerthal	Glaubzahl
Eduardsthal	Hasenböhl

10

Ziegelhohl	Grund-Schwalheim
Hoxhohl	Ingelheim
Hähnleinhoxhohl	Ober-Ingelheim
Pohl	Nieder-Ingelheim
Rad-Mühl	Heuchelheim
-Hof, Mühl	Gau-Bickelheim
Holz-Mühl	Gau-Böckelheim
Wetzkeil	Leiselheim
Dortelweil	Wahlheim
Petterweil	Hangen-Wahlheim
Bußfell	Fehlheim
-Hof, Hell	Mühlheim
Zell	Saulheim
Echzell	Ober-Saulheim
Gill	Nieder-Saulheim
Stoll	Stammheim
Nieder-Stoll	Schwanheim
Güll	Abenheim
Hof-Güll	Schwabenheim
Dorf-Güll	Pfaffen-Schwabenheim
Homberg an der Ohm	Sauber-Schwabenheim
Radheim	Laubenheim
Lindheim	Bubenheim
Gundheim	Badenheim
Rodheim	Undenheim
Nordheim	Bodenheim
Leeheim	Udenheim
Seeheim	Budenheim
Schaafheim	Offenheim
Hofheim	Bingenheim
Hospital Hofheim	Jugenheim
Heegheim	Bechenheim
Pfiffligheim	Muschenheim
Bergheim	Dienheim
Wald-Bergheim	Beienheim
Langen-Bergheim	Hackenheim
Hochheim	Mackenheim
Horchheim	Nackenheim
Bauschheim	Ockenheim
Stockheim	Bockenheim
Dürkheim	Stein-Bockenheim
Rhein-Dürkheim	Flockenheim
Dorn-Dürkheim	Sporkenheim
Dalheim	Mommenheim
Schwalheim	Rumpenheim

Appenheim	Viernheim
Heppenheim	Wackernheim
Klein-Heppenheim	Mommernheim
Gau-Heppenheim	Winternheim
Oppenheim	Klein-Winternheim
Kloppenheim	Groß-Winternheim
Wies-Oppenheim	Bauernheim
Friesenheim	Dauernheim
Gonsenheim	Ober-Dauernheim
Bosenheim	Monzernheim
Assenheim	Bornheim
Massenheim	Dornheim
Dorn-Assenheim	Zornheim
Essenheim	Raunheim
Ossenheim	Harheim
Partenheim	Rohrheim
Wattenheim	Klein-Rohrheim
Kettenheim	Ober-Rohrheim
Mettenheim	Groß-Rohrheim
Frettenheim	Dorheim
Dautenheim	Gabsheim
Bretzenheim	Gimbsheim
Zotzenheim	Biebesheim
Hahnheim	Heidesheim
Lehnheim	Blödesheim
Reinheim	Büdesheim
Rohrbach bei Reinheim	Bingen-Büdesheim
Steinheim	Erbes-Büdesheim
Klein-Steinheim	Algesheim
Ober-Steinheim	Gau-Algesheim
Nieder-Steinheim	Welgesheim
Groß-Steinheim	Dolgesheim
Weinheim	Jügesheim
Frei-Weinheim	Spiesheim
Nieder-Weinheim	Griesheim
Gau-Weinheim	Weckesheim
Zeppelinheim	Hillesheim
Biebelnheim	Ippesheim
Flonheim	Dietesheim
Gadernheim	Dintesheim
Odernheim	Wolfsheim
Gau-Odernheim	Bischofsheim
Köngernheim	Main-Bischofsheim
Bös-Köngernheim	Gau-Bischofsheim
Gau-Köngernheim	Kriegsheim

Weisheim

Hangen-Weisheim

Aspisheim

Alsheim

Dalsheim

Walsheim

Elsheim

Biebelsheim

Wendelsheim

Düdelsheim

Rudelsheim

Reichelsheim

Eckelsheim

Eppelsheim

Wisselsheim

Gosselsheim

Rüsselsheim

Dittelsheim

Mölsheim

Weinolsheim

Grolsheim

Bechtolsheim

Gaulsheim

Eimsheim

Schimsheim

Armsheim

Ensheim

Bensheim

Rodau bei Bensheim

Geinsheim

Weinsheim

Ginsheim

Lonsheim

Monsheim

Sponsheim

Wonsheim

Gernsheim

Schornsheim

Herrnsheim

Ebersheim

Ibersheim

Hilbersheim

Ober-Hilbersheim

Nieder-Hilbersheim

Laubersheim

Frei-Laubersheim

Eddersheim

Pfeddersheim

Wüsten-Eddersheim

Klein-Eddersheim

Widdersheim

Ober-Widdersheim

Nieder-Widdersheim

Unter-Widdersheim

Vendersheim

Siefersheim

Wölfersheim

Bellersheim

Framersheim

Heimersheim

Freimersheim

Nieder-Freimersheim

Rommersheim

Dromersheim

Bermersheim

Dietersheim

Pleitersheim

Wintersheim

Uelversheim

Wald-Uelversheim

Ilversheim

Ülversheim

Flörsheim

Ober-Flörsheim

Nieder-Flörsheim

Straßheim

Bechtheim

Altheim

Spitzaltheim

Wallertheim

Lampertheim

Astheim

Hechstheim

Ostheim

Kostheim

Trautheim

Auheim

Nauheim

Bad Nauheim

Klein-Auheim

Dexheim	Knoden
Volxheim	Roden
Harxheim	Ober-Roden
Gorxheim	Nieder-Roden
Welzheim	Achtstauden
Klein-Welzheim	Gleen
Holzheim	Ober-Gleen
Sulzheim	Freien-Seen
Enzheim	Pfaffen
Habitzheim	Olfen
-Hof, Helm	Uffhofen
Olm	Dudenhofen
Ober-Olm	Pfaffenhofen
Nieder-Olm	Sickenhofen
Woogsdamm	Frohnhofen
Hamm	Obbornhofen
Heusenstamm	Dilshofen
Tromm	Oppershofen
Guntersblum	Allertshofen
Etzean	Westhofen
Bieben	Ernsthofen
Iben	Osthofen
Karben	Kalkofen
Klein-Karben	Zipfen
Groß-Karben	Wimpfen
Staden	Bad Wimpfen
Langwaden	Rödgen
Kohden	Schlechtenwegen
Inheiden	-Hof, Selgen
Ofleiden	Arheilgen
Ober-Ofleiden	-Hof, Silgen
Nieder-Ofleiden	Hangen
Rheinfelden	Langen
Erfelden	Bingen
Beerfelden	Köddingen
Mörfelden	Büdingen
Worfelden	Sprendlingen
Burkhardsfelden	Mainflingen
Linden	Klingen
-Hof, Linden	Buchklingen
Großen-Linden	Kuh-Klingen
Klein-Linden	Mühlklingen
Gemünden	Guldenklingen
Burg Gemünden	Lichtenklingen
Nieder-Gemünden	Hainzenklingen

Ober-Klingen
Nieder-Klingen
Gertelsklingen
Hiltersklingen
Ober-Hiltersklingen
Unter-Hiltersklingen
Villingen
Grüningen
Hoingen
Höingen
Daubringen
Gensingen
Bessingen
Ober-Bessingen
Nieder-Bessingen
Hungen
Flensungen
Bessungen
Salzungen
Bad Salzungen
Bergen
Heldenbergen
Heckenbergen
Hundertmorgen
Rinderbügen
Kaichen
Eichen
Klein-Eichen
Unter-Eichen
Groß-Eichen
Richen
Malchen
Hainchen
Ruhlkirchen
Beedenkirchen
Neunkirchen
Reiskirchen
Weiskirchen
Gonterskirchen
Hitzkirchen
Achtbuchen
Finthen
Freien
-Hof, Marien
Stadecken

Leidhecken
-Hof, Hecken
Spachbrücken
Eschollbrücken
Rembrücken
Bruchenbrücken
Feldkrücken
Falken
-Hof, Falken
-Hof, Finken
Wahlen
Wolfskehlen
Mörlen
Ober-Mörlen
Nieder-Mörlen
Aulen
Seemen
Mittel-Seemen
Ober-Seemen
Nieder-Seemen
Zahmen
Ohmen
Ober-Ohmen
Nieder-Ohmen
Dirlammen
Hemmen
Schönnen
-Aue, Nonnen
-Hof, Nonnen
Gumpen
Kleingumpen
Klein-Gumpen
Ober-Kleingumpen
Groß-Gumpen
Saasen
Königsaasen
Wettsaasen
Wiesen
-Hof, Wiesen
Breitenwiesen
Nieder-Wiesen
Bindsachsen
Eichelsachsen
Mühlsachsen
Reisen

Sassen	Ruthardshausen
Jugenheim in Rheinhessen	Ilbeshausen
Gießen	Orleshausen
Hausen	Harreshausen
Waldhausen	Rüddingshausen
Windhausen	Ehringshausen
Schafhausen	Ettingshausen
Froschhausen	Ringelshausen
Kirschhausen	Oppelshausen
Utschhausen	Geilshausen
Stockhausen	Elmshausen
Balkhausen	Wilmshausen
Friedelhausen	Bernshausen
Igelhausen	Wäldershausen
Rommelhausen	Wingershausen
Mühlhausen	Hergershausen
Wallhausen	Üllershausen
Zellhausen	Uppershausen
Babenhausen	Patershausen
Bobenhausen	Gontershausen
Erbenhausen	Guntershausen
Landenhausen	Hartershausen
Odenhausen	Mittershausen
Udenhausen	Ruttershausen
Gräfenhausen	Groß-Hausen
Georgenhausen	Eckartshausen
Sichenhausen	Schwickartshausen
Frankenhausen	Einartshausen
Schneppenhausen	Rabertshausen
Messenhausen	Heibertshausen
Bettenhausen	Obertshausen
Hainhausen	Allertshausen
Einhausen	Billertshausen
Klein-Hausen	Heimertshausen
Schellnhausen	Eppertshausen
Illnhausen	Oppertshausen
Kolnhausen	Harpertshausen
Schönhausen	Schmittshausen
Vonhausen	Lusthausen
Obernhausen	Neuhausen
Niedernhausen	Wixhausen
Gundernhausen	Salzhausen
Wallernhausen	Holzhausen
Haarhausen	Burgholzhausen
Neckar-Hausen	Erzhausen

Ützhausen
Königstädten
Hochstädten
Wallerstädten
Weiten
Zwiefalten
Kempten
Hopfgarten
Kirschgarten
Baumgarten
Rosengarten
Thiergarten
Tiergarten
Wolfsgarten
Forstgarten
Winterkasten
Wüsten
Schmitten
Ober-Schmitten
Unter-Schmitten
Schotten
Glashütten
Lauten
Ywen
-Hof, Layen
Selzen
Sülzen
Hohen-Sülzen
Etzen
Gietzen
Götzen
Wildbahn
Hahn
Allendorf an der Lahn
Hain
Windhain
Eichelhain
Grebenhain
Greifenhain
Langenhain
Dreieichenhain
Herchenhain
Gleimenhain
Altenhain
Kölzenhain

Lanzenhain
Hirzenhain
Atzenhain
Götzenhain
Reinhardshain
Rebgeshain
Breungeshain
Rudingshain
Bermuthshain
Eckmannshain
Hartmannshain
Arnshain
Helpershain
Weitershain
Beltershain
Vaitshain
Weickartshain
Volkartshain
Streithain
Weitzhain
Main
Offenbach am Main
Mühlheim am Main
Schützenrain
Eich am Rhein
Laubenheim am Rhein
Steinheim am Rhein
Stein am Rhein
-Hof, Klein
Hähnlein
Grein
Herbstein
Offstein
Kranichstein
Ulrichstein
Neu-Ulrichstein
Böllstein
Wöllstein
Mulstein
Raubenstein
Rodenstein
Hohenstein
Frankenstein
Weißenstein
Nierstein

Winterstein	Uhlerborn
Borstein	Sandbach-Uhlerborn
-Hof, Schelln	Eckartsborn
St. Johann	Dorn
Sankt Johann	Hirschhorn
Langgewann	Rimhorn
Vielbrunn	Geinhaar
Asselbrunn	Gelnhaar
Breitenbrunn	Maar
Hainbrunn	Birklar
Ober-Hainbrunn	Lollar
Unter-Hainbrunn	Mainzlar
Schönbrunn	Hof, Hainaer
Siedelsbrunn	Bieber
Sion	Offenbach-Bieber
Webern	Sauber
Gadern	Höchst an der Nidder
Gedern	Hof, Arnheider
Geudern	Jungenfelder
Hörgern	Hof, Altenfelder
Ober-Hörgern	Hof, Sensfelder
Zimmern	Hof, Olfer
Klein-Zimmern	-Hof, Wolfer
Groß-Zimmern	Hof, Altdörfer
Mit-Lechtern	-Hof, Jäger
Alt-Lechtern	Aue, Königsklinger
Leihgestern	Hof, Flensunger
Ostern	Hof, Fengenberger
Ober-Ostern	Hof, Kahlenberger
Unter-Ostern	Hof, Wiesberger
Lautern	Hof, Vogelsberger
Seckmauern	Hof, Steckelsberger
Beuern	Hof, Vöckelsberger
Born	Hof, Albacher
Frischborn	hof, Kröckelbacher
Queckborn	Hof, Erbacher
Esselborn	Hof, Laubacher
Büttelborn	Hof, Westphälischer
Rimborn	Hof, Preußischer
Flomborn	Hof, Falkscher
Marienborn	Hof, Geygerscher
Appenborn	Hof, Roosscher
Usenborn	Hof, Haxenbucher
Busenborn	Weiher
Watzenborn	Fischweiher

Bonsweiher

Mähacker

Steinacker

Hof, Grünhecker

Hof, Birker

Hof, Biedenthaler

Hof, Rauenthaler

Hof, Dorndieler

Langklingler

Horrweiler

Banzweiler

Lörzweiler

Hof, Aechzeller

-Hof, Krämer

Hof, Rodheimer

Hof, Bischheimer

Hof, Münchbischheimer

Hof, Schwalheimer

Hof, Wahlheimer

Hof, Staudenheimer

Hof, Bockenheimer

Hof, Bettenheimer

Hof, Heyenheimer

Hof, Bonnheimer

Hof, Bornheimer

Hof, Bensheimer

Hof, Gommersheimer

Hof, Oberstraßheimer

Hof, Boxheimer

Hammer

Georgenhammer

Luisenhammer

Hessenbrücker Hammer

Mühlhäuser Hammer

Unter-Hammer

Obernseener

Hof, Oberseener

Hof, Hainer

Hof, Bollhainer

Hof, Petershainer

Hof, Gehaborner

Hof, Treburer

Hof, Breitwieser

Langwasser

Hof, Riedhäuser

Windhäuser

Hof, Häuser

Hof, Stockhäuser

Hof, Retschenhäuser

Hof, Mückenhäuser

Reinhäuser

Hof, Wellershäuser

Hof, Karthäuser

Hof,Haxthäuser

Hof, Darmstädter

Schlichter

Münster

Lautern

Hof, Ringauer

Hof, Remayer

-Hof, Mayer

-Hof, Geyer

Böllenfallthor

Jägertor

Dürr

Trebur

Gras

Harras

Burkhards

Hof, Beinhards

-Hof, Leonhards

Erbes

Lindes

Schadges

Röthges

-Hof, Tönges

Wernges

Eiches

Meiches

Büches

Orles

Ohmes

-Hof, Vietmes

-Hof, Steines

-Hof, Grünes

Oes

Bisses

Nauses

Ober-Nauses

Schloß-Nauses

Sandlofs	Weiten-Gesäß
-Hof, Schlieglofs	Etzen-Gesäß
Willofs	Bös-Gesäß
Billings	Geiß
Wenings	-Hof, Geiß
Wernings	Marienschloß
Kernbachs	Neuschloß
Lais	Kaulstoß
Ober-Lais	Nösberts
Unter-Lais	Steigerts
Drais	Bücherts
Trais	-Hof, Rückerts
Treis	Wehnerts
Biblis	Hollahaus
-Hof, Johannis	Waldhaus
Lindenfels	Markhaus
Stornfels	Wehrzollhaus
-Hof, Karls	Leimenhaus
Solms	Hainhaus
Worms	Jägerhaus
Getürms	Hühnerhaus
Göns	Westerhaus
Lang-Göns	Falltorhaus
Kirch-Göns	Glitzenhorner Falltorhaus
Pohl-Göns	Rohrs-Haus
Bös	Messeler Forsthaus
Heblos	Bingenheimer Forsthaus
Wasserbiblos	Neuhaus
Rudlos	Wiedermus
Reichlos	Alt-Wiedermus
Rimlos	Steinbach am Taunus
Merlos	Hubertus
Metzlos	Bobstadt
Moos	Kleestadt
Weid-Moos	Langstadt
Nösberts-Weidmoos	Pfungstadt
Wünschen-Moos	Eich bei Pfungstadt
Ober-Moos	Hahn bei Pfungstadt
Nieder-Moos	Mochstadt
-Hof, Hoppers	Wickstadt
Selters	Ockstadt
Heisters	Mockstadt
Reuters	Ober-Mockstadt
Graß	Nieder-Mockstadt
Falken-Gesäß	Stockstadt

Engelstadt	Freiheit
Michelstadt	Laudenau-Freiheit
Kallstadt	Hiltersklingen an der Hart
Wöllstadt	Momart
Ober-Wöllstadt	Hohewart
Nieder-Wöllstadt	-Hof, Wart
Ramstadt	Birkert
Ober-Ramstadt	Heidenfahrt
Nieder-Ramstadt	Gernsheimer Fahrt
Darmstadt	Steinfurt
Traisa bei Darmstadt	Höchst
Umstadt	Horst
Klein-Umstadt	Günterfürst
Crumstadt	Luisenlust
Krumstadt	Jägerlust
Groß-Umstadt	Wüst
Ranstadt	-Hof, Schmitt
Ilbenstadt	Steinkaut
Nieder-Ilbenstadt	Au
Seligenstadt	Brandau
Hohenstadt	Mittel-Gründau
Altenstadt	Hain-Gründau
Hainstadt	Modau
Bönstadt	Ober-Modau
Berstadt	Nieder-Modau
Eberstadt	Rodau
Koberstadt	Benzelsche Au
Hanauer Koberstadt	-Hof, Au
Kocherstadt	Gau
Weiterstadt	Stockau
Florstadt	Goddelau
Ober-Florstadt	Michelau
Nieder-Florstadt	Kisselau
Unter-Florstadt	Bullau
Mörstadt	Wald-Bullau
Wörrstadt	Erlau
Bürstadt	Merlau
Leustadt	Rabenau
Neustadt	Liebenau
Moxstadt	Grebenau
-Hof, Schardt	Laudenau
Braunshardt	Hörgenau
Pfordt	Rauchenau
Burgbracht	Hohenau
Burg Bracht	Birkenau

Weisenau	Mossau
Hartenau	Ober-Mossau
Fürstenau	Unter-Mossau
Gettenau	Alzey
Gunzenau	-Aue, Lothary
Steinau	Salz
Freien-Steinau	Buchholz
Michelnau	Vorholz
Schönau	Gersprenz
Gronau	Ober-Gersprenz
Bieberau	Unter-Gersprenz
Klein-Bieberau	Mainz
Groß-Bieberau	Schwarz
Oberau	Unter-Schwarz
Überau	Schlitz
Gerau	Weschnitz
Klein-Gerau	Lauten-Weschnitz
Groß-Gerau	Gehspitz
Unterau	Merkenfritz
Reichelsheim in der Wetterau	Heiligkreuz
Ludwigsau	Reisenkreuz
Petersau	Habermannskreuz
Wersau	

Typical *Fachwek*
architecture in Hesse

Alphabetical Index of the Grand Duchy of Hesse

Abenheim
Absteinach
Abtsteinach
Achtbuchen
Achtstauden
Aechzeller Hof
Affhöllerbach
Affolterbach
Airlenbach
Albach
Albacher Hof
Albersbach
Albertsruhe
Albig
Algesheim
Allendorf an der Lahn
Allendorf an der Lumda
Allenrod
Allertshausen
Allertshofen
Allmendfeld
Allmenrod
Alsbach
Alsfeld
Alsheim
Alt-Lechtern
Alt-Wiedermus
Altdörfer Hof
Alte Sandaue
Alten-Buseck
Altenburg
Altenfelder Hof
Altenhain
Altensand
Altenschlirf
Altenstadt
Altheim
Alzey
Amalienhof
Amöneburg
Amorbach

Angelhof
Angenrod
Angersbach
Annelsbach
Annerod
Antoniusberg
Apfelbachbrücke
Appenborn
Appenheim
Appenrod
Arheilgen
Armsheim
Arnheider Hof
Arnsburg
Arnshain
Asbach
Aschbach
Aspisheim
Asselbrunn
Assenheim
Astheim
Atzenhain
Au
Au-Hof
Au-Hof
Auerbach
auf dem Loh
Auheim
Aulen
Aulen-Diebach
Babenhausen
Bad Salzungen
Bad Nauheim
Bad Wimpfen
Badenburg
Badenheim
Balkhausen
Balsbach
Bamberg
Bannerod
Banzweiler

Bastelshof
Bauernheim
Baumgarten
Bauschheim
Bechenheim
Bechtheim
Bechtolsheim
Beedenkirchen
Beerbach
Beerfelden
Beerfurth
Beienheim
Beinhards Hof
Bellersheim
Bellmuth
Beltershain
Bensheim
Bensheimer Hof
Benzelsche Au
Bergen
Bergheim
Berkach
Bermersheim
Bermuthshain
Berngeroth
Bernsburg
Bernsfeld
Bernshausen
Bersrod
Berstadt
Bessingen
Bessungen
Bettenbach
Bettenhausen
Bettenheimer Hof
Betzenrod
Beuern
Beunde Hof
Beyerseich
Biblis
Bickenbach
Biebelnheim
Biebelsheim
Bieben
Bieber

Bieberau
Bieberberg
Biebesheim
Biedenthaler Hof
Bierbach
Billertshausen
Billings
Bindsachsen
Bing
Bingen
Bingen-Büdesheim
Bingenheim
Bingenheimer Forsthaus
Birkenau
Birker Hof
Birkert
Birklar
Bischheimer Hof
Bischofsheim
Bisses
Blei-Aue
Bleichenbach
Bleidenrod
Blitzenrod
Blödesheim
Blofeld
Bobenhausen
Bobstadt
Bockenheim
Bockenheimer Hof
Bockenrod
Bodenheim
Bodenrod
Böllenfallthor
Bollhainer Hof
Bollnbach
Böllstein
Bonnheimer Hof
Bönstadt
Bonsweiher
Born
Bornheim
Bornheimer Hof
Borsdorf
Borstein

Bös
Bös-Gesäß
Bös-Köngernheim
Bosenheim
Boxheimer Hof
Brandau
Brauerschwend
Braunshardt
Breidenbach
Breitenbach
Breitenbrunn
Breitenhaide
Breitenloh
Breitenwiesen
Breitwieser Hof
Bremhof
Brensbach
Bretzenheim
Breuberg
Breungeshain
Brombach
Brometsberg
Bruchenbrücken
Bruchhof
Brunnthal
Bubenheim
Bücherts
Büches
Buchholz
Buchklingen
Buchschlag
Budenheim
Büdesheim
Büdingen
Bullau
Burg Gemünden
Burg Breuberg
Burg Bracht
Burg Gräfenrode
Burgbracht
Bürgel
Burghof
Burgholzhausen
Burkhards
Burkhardsfelden

Bürstadt
Buseck
Busenborn
Büßfeld
Bußfell
Büttelborn
Butzbach
Calbach
Christinenhof
Claraberg
Climbach
Consdorf
Corsica
Crainfeld
Crumbach
Crumstadt
Dalheim
Dalsheim
Dammeshof
Dannenrod
Darmstadt
Darmstädter Hof
Darsberg
Daubringen
Dauernheim
Dautenheim
Deckenbach
Dexheim
Dianaburg
Diebach am Haag
Diebach
Dieburg
Dienheim
Dietersheim
Dietesheim
Dietzenbach
Dilshofen
Dintesheim
Dippelshof
Dirlammen
Dittelsheim
Dolgesheim
Dorf-Erbach
Dorf-Güll
Dorheim

Dorn
Dorn-Assenheim
Dorn-Dürkheim
Dornberg
Dorndiel
Dorndieler Hof
Dornheim
Dortelweil
Dotzelrod
Drais
Dreieichenhain
Dromersheim
Düdelsheim
Dudenhofen
Dudenrod
Dürkheim
Dürr
Dürr-Ellenbach
Dusenbach
Eberbach
Ebersberg
Ebersheim
Eberstadt
Echzell
Eckartsborn
Eckartshausen
Eckelsheim
Eckmannshain
Eddersheim
Eduardsthal
Effolderbach
Egelfurth
Egelsbach
Ehringshausen
Eich am Rhein
Eich bei Pfungstadt
Eichelberg
Eichelhain
Eichelsachsen
Eichelsdorf
Eichen
Eichenrod
Eiches
Eichloch
Eifa

Eimsheim
Einartshausen
Einhausen
Einsiedel
Eisenbach
Eiserne Hand
Elbenrod
Ellenbach
Elmshausen
Elpenrod
Elsbach
Elsheim
Emelinenhütte
Engelhof
Engelrod
Engelstadt
Engelthal
Ensheim
Enzheim
Eppelsheim
Eppertshausen
Erbach
Erbacher Hof
Erbenhausen
Erbes
Erbes-Büdesheim
Erbuch
Erfelden
Erlau
Erlenbach
Ermenrod
Ernsbach
Ernsthofen
Erzbach
Erzhausen
Eschbach
Eschenrod
Eschollbrücken
Esselborn
Essenheim
Ettingshausen
Etzean
Etzen
Etzen-Gesäß
Eudorf

Eulbach
Eulenhof
Eulersdorf
Eulsbach
Eutergrund
Fahrenbach
Falken
Falken-Gesäß
Falken-Hof
Falkscher Hof
Falltorhaus
Fängenhof
Fasanerie
Fauerbach bei Nidda
Fauerbach vor der Höhe
Faustenbach
Fehlheim
Felda
Feldkrücken
Felsberg
Fengenberger Hof
Finken-Hof
Finkenbach
Finkenloch
Finthen
Fischweiher
Flensungen
Flensunger Hof
Fleschenbach
Flockenbach
Flockenbusch
Flockenheim
Flomborn
Flonheim
Flörsheim
Florstadt
Forstel
Forstgarten
Framersheim
Frankel
Frankenfeld
Frankenhausen
Frankenstein
Fränkisch-Crumbach
Frau-Rombach

Frauenhecke
Frei-Laubersheim
Frei-Weinheim
Freien
Freien-Seen
Freien-Steinau
Freiheit
Freimersheim
Frettenheim
Friedberg
Friedberg-Fauerbach
Friedelhausen
Friedrichsburg
Friedrichshütte
Friesenheim
Frischborn
Frohnhofen
Fronhof
Fronkelsgrund
Froschhausen
Fulder Aue
Fürfeld
Fürstenau
Fürstengrund
Fürth
Gabsheim
Gadern
Gadernheim
Galmbach
Gambach
Gammelsbach
Ganseburg
Garbenteich
Gaßbach
Gau
Gau-Algesheim
Gau-Bickelheim
Gau-Bischofsheim
Gau-Böckelheim
Gau-Heppenheim
Gau-Köngernheim
Gau-Odernheim
Gau-Weinheim
Gaulsheim
Gebhardshütte

Gedern
Gehaborner Hof
Gehag
Gehspitz
Geilshausen
Geinhaar
Geinsheim
Geiß
Geiß-Hof
Geiß-Nidda
Geisberg
Geisenbach
Gelnhaar
Gemünden
Gensingen
Georgenhammer
Georgenhausen
Gerau
Gernsheim
Gernsheimer Fahrt
Gersprenz
Gertelsklingen
Gettenau
Getürms
Geudern
Geyer-Hof
Geygerscher Hof
Gießen
Gietzen
Gill
Gimbsheim
Ginsheim
Ginsheim-Gustavsburg
Glashütte
Glashütten
Glattbach
Glauberg
Glaubzahl
Gleen
Gleimenhain
Glitzenhorner Falltorhaus
Göbelnrod
Goddelau
Gommersheimer Hof
Göns

Gonsenheim
Gontershausen
Gonterskirchen
Gorxheim
Gosselsheim
Götzen
Götzenhain
Gräbenbruch
Grafenbruch
Gräfenhausen
Gras
Graß
Gras-Ellenbach
Grebenau
Grebenhain
Greifenhain
Grein
Griedel
Griesheim
Grolsheim
Gronau
Groß-Bieberau
Groß-Breitenbach
Groß-Eichen
Groß-Gerau
Groß-Gumpen
Groß-Hausen
Groß-Karben
Groß-Rohrheim
Groß-Steinheim
Groß-Umstadt
Groß-Winternheim
Groß-Zimmern
Großen-Buseck
Großen-Linden
Großendorf
Grube Messel
Grubenbach
Grünberg
Grund
Grund-Schwalheim
Grundhause
Grünes-Hof
Grünhecker Hof
Grüningen

Guldenklingen
Güll
Gumpen
Gumpersberg
Gundernhausen
Gundheim
Gundhof
Günterfürst
Guntersblum
Guntershausen
Gunzenau
Gustavsburg
Güttersbach
Haarhausen
Haberich
Habermannskreuz
Habitzheim
Hackenheim
Hahn bei Pfungstadt
Hahnheim
Hähnlein
Hähnleinhoxhohl
Hain
Hain in der Dreieich
Hain-Gründau
Hainaer Hof
Hainbach
Hainbrunn
Hainchen
Hainer Hof
Haingrund
Hainhaus
Hainhausen
Hainstadt
Hainzenklingen
Haisterbach
Hambach
Hamm
Hammelbach
Hammelburg
Hämmelsbach
Hammer
Hanauer Koberstadt
Hangen
Hangen-Wahlheim

Hangen-Weisheim
Harbach
Harbwald
Hardthof
Harheim
Harpertshausen
Harras
Harreshausen
Hartenau
Hartenrod
Hartershausen
Hartmannshain
Harxheim
Hasenböhl
Haßloch
Hässel
Hassel-Hof
Hasselberg
Hasselhag
Hasselheck
Hassenroth
Hattenrod
Hausen
Hausen am Hausberg
Häuser Hof
Haxenbucher Hof
Haxthäuser Hof
Hayna
Heblos
Hebstahl
Hechstheim
Hecken-Hof
Hecken-Hof
Heckenbergen
Heckenhof
Heckersdorf
Heegheim
Heibertshausen
Heide
Heidelbach
Heidenfahrt
Heidenhof
Heidesheim
Heiligenberg
Heiligkreuz

Heimersheim
Heimertshausen
Heisters
Heldenbergen
Hellenhütte
Helm-Hof
Helmsberg
Helpershain
Hembach
Hemmen
Hengmantel
Henriettenhof
Heppenheim an der Bergstraße
Heppenheim an der Wiese
Heppenheim im Loch
Herberge-Hof
Herbstein
Herchenhain
Herchenrode
Hergersdorf
Hergershausen
Hering
Herrenhof
Herrnhaag
Herrnsheim
Heßloch
Hesselbach
Hessenaue
Hessenbrücker Hammer
Hetschbach
Hetzbach
Heubach
Heuberg
Heuchelheim
Heusenstamm
Hexthäuser Hof
Heyenheimer Hof
Hilbersheim
Hillesheim
Hilsig-Hof
Hiltersklingen an der Hart
Himbach
Hinterbach
Hippelsbach
Hirschhorn

Hirzenhain
Hitzkirchen
Hoch-Weisel
Hochheim
Höchst an der Nidder
Höchst im Odenwald
Hochstädten
Höckersdorf
Hof
Hof-Güll
Hofheim im Ried
Hohberg
Hohen-Sülzen
Hohenau
Hohenhäuserhof
Hohenstadt
Hohenstein
Hohewart
Hoingen
Höingen
Hollahaus
Höllerbach
Höllerhecke
Höllhof
Holmbach
Holz-Mühl
Holzhausen
Holzheim
Holzwiese
Homberg
Homberg an der Ohm
Hopfgarten
Hopfmannsfeld
Hoppers-Hof
Horchheim
Hörgenau
Hörgern
Horloff
Hornbach
Horrweiler
Horst
Hospital Hofheim
Hospital Hof
Hospital-Hof
Hottenbach

Hotzberg
Hoxhohl
Hubertus
Huckenhof
Hühnerhaus
Hummetroth
Hundertmorgen
Hungen
Hüttenberg
Hüttenfeld
Hüttenthal
Hutzdorf
Hutzwiese
Iben
Ibersheim
Igelhausen
Igelsbach
Ilbenstadt
Ilbeshausen
Illbach
Illnhausen
Ilsdorf
Ilversheim
im Steinbickel
im Windloch
in der Straßburg
Ingelheim
Inheiden
Ippesheim
Isenburg
Jäger-Hof
Jägerhaus
Jägerlust
Jägersburg
Jägerthal
Jägertor
Jakobsberg
Jakobsberger Aue
Johannis-Hof
Johannisberg
Jugenheim an der Bergstraße
Jugenheim in Rheinhessen
Jügesheim
Juhöhe
Jungenfelder

Kaffeeberg
Kahlenberger Hof
Kaichen
Kailbach
Kainsbach
Kaisergrube
Kälberteich
Kalkofen
Kallstadt
Kammerhof
Kannengießerhechenhof
Karben
Karls-Hof
Karthäuser Hof
Kastel
Kaulstoß
Kefenrod
Kellersberg
Kelsterbach
Kempten
Kernbach
Kernbachs
Kernbachs-Hütte
Kesselbach
Kestrich
Kettenheim
Kiliansherberge
Kilsbach
Kimbach
Kinzig
Kirch-Beerfurth
Kirch-Brombach
Kirch-Göns
Kirchberg
Kirschgarten
Kirschhausen
Kirtorf
Kisselau
Kisselau-Wörth
Kleestadt
Klein-Auheim
Klein-Bieberau
Klein-Breitenbach
Klein-Eddersheim
Klein-Eichen

Klein-Ellenbach
Klein-Felda
Klein-Gerau
Klein-Gumpen
Klein-Hausen
Klein-Heppenheim
Klein-Hof
Klein-Karben
Klein-Krotzenburg
Klein-Linden
Klein-Lumda
Klein-Rohrheim
Klein-Steinheim
Klein-Umstadt
Klein-Welzheim
Klein-Winternheim
Klein-Zimmern
Kleingumpen
Klimbach
Klingen
Kloppenheim
Knoblochsaue
Knoden
Koberstadt
Kocherbach
Kocherstadt
Kochertsberg
Köddingen
Kohden
Kohlberg
Kohlgrube
Kohlwiese
Kolmbach
Kolnhausen
Kölzenhain
Köngernheim
König
Königsaasen
Königsklinger Aue
Königstädten
Konradsdorf
Kornsand
Korsika
Kortelshütte
Kostheim

Krähenberg
Krainfeld
Krämer-Hof
Kranichstein
Krausebuche
Kreidach
Kreiswald
Kreutzersgrund
Kreuzburg
Kriegsheim
Kröckelbach
Kröckelbacher Hof
Kröckelbacher Hof
Krötenburg
Krotzenburg
Krumbach
Krumstadt
Kuh
Kuh-Klingen
Kühkopf
Kuhruhe
Kunnebach
Kunzenbach
Kuralpe Kreuzhof
Lache
Lais
Lämmerspiel
Lampertheim
Landenhausen
Lang
Lang-Aue
Lang-Göns
Langd
Langen
Langen-Bergheim
Langen-Brombach
Langenhain
Langenthal
Langgewann
Langklingler
Langstadt
Langwaden
Langwasser
Lanzenbach
Lanzenhain

Lardenbach
Laubach
Laubacher Hof
Laubacher Wald
Laubenheim am Rhein
Laubersheim
Laudenau
Laudenau-Freiheit
Laurenzberg
Lauten
Lauten-Weschnitz
Lauterbach
Lautern
Lautern
Layen-Hof
Leberbach
Lebertsaue
Leeheim
Lehnheim
Lehrbach
Leidhecken
Leihgestern
Leimenhaus
Leiselheim
Lempelstieg
Lengfeld
Leonhards-Hof
Lerchenhof
Leuerbach
Leusel
Leustadt
Lich
Lichtenberg
Lichtenklingen
Liebenau
Liebersbach
Liebfrauenthal
Liedenbach
Liederbach
Linden
Linden-Hof
Lindenberg
Lindenfels
Lindenstruth
Lindes

Lindheim
Linnenbach
Lißberg
Litzard
Litzelbach
Lohhof
Löhrbach
Lollar
Londorf
Lonsheim
Lorbach
Lorsch
Lorscher Wald
Lörzenbach
Lörzweiler
Lothary-Aue
Lotzenbuckel
Löwenhof
Löwenruhe
Löwenthal
Ludwigsau
Ludwigsdorf
Ludwigshöhe
Ludwigshütte
Luisenhammer
Luisenlust
Lumda
Lusthausen
Lützel-Rimbach
Lützel-Wiebelsbach
Lützelbach
Maar
Mackenheim
Mähacker
Maibach
Main-Bischofsheim
Mainflingen
Mainz
Mainzisch-Crumbach
Mainzlar
Malchen
Maltheserhof
Mangelhof
Mangelsbach
Marbach

Maria
Maria-Einsiedel
Marien-Hof
Marienberg
Marienborn
Marienhöhe
Marienschloß
Markhaus
Massenheim
Maulbach
Maulbeeraue
Mayer-Hof
Meiches
Melbach
Melchiorsgrund
Melsbach
Mengelbach
Merkenfritz
Merlau
Merlos
Meßbach
Messel
Messeler Forsthaus
Messenhausen
Mettenheim
Metzlos
Metzlos-Gehag
Michelau
Michelbach
Michelnau
Michelstadt
Minchbach
Mit-Lechtern
Mittel-Gründau
Mittel-Kinzig
Mittel-Seemen
Mitteldick
Mittershausen
Mittlerer Busch
Mochstadt
Mockstadt
Modau
Mölsheim
Momart
Mombach

Mommenheim
Mommernheim
Mönchbruch
Mönchhof
Mönchsbach
Mönchshöfe
Monsheim
Monzernheim
Moos
Mörfelden
Mörfelden-Gundhof
Mörlen
Mörlenbach
Mörstadt
Mosbach
Mossau
Moxstadt
Mücke
Mückenhäuser Hof
Mühl-Hof
Mühlhausen
Mühlhäuser Hammer
Mühlheim am Main
Mühlklingen
Mühlsachsen
Mühlwörth
Mulstein
Mumbach
Mümling
Mummenroth
Münch
Münch-Leusel
Münchbischheimer Hof
Münschbach
Münster
Münzenberg
Muschenheim
Nack
Nackenheim
Nauheim
Nauheimer Oberwald
Nauses
Neckar-Hausen
Neckar-Liebersbach
Neckar-Steinach

Neu-Bamberg
Neu-Isenburg
Neu-Kelsterbach
Neu-Ulrichstein
Neuburg
Neudorf
Neuhaus
Neuhausen
Neuhof
Neunkirchen
Neuschloß
Neustadt
Neuthal
Neutsch
Neuwerk
Nidda
Niedendorf
Nieder-Beerbach
Nieder-Bessingen
Nieder-Breidenbach
Nieder-Erlenbach
Nieder-EschFischbach
Nieder-Flörsheim
Nieder-Florstadt
Nieder-Freimersheim
Nieder-Gemünden
Nieder-Hilbersheim
Nieder-Ilbenstadt
Nieder-Ingelheim
Nieder-kainsbach
Nieder-Kinzig
Nieder-Klingen
Nieder-Liebersbach
Nieder-Mockstadt
Nieder-Modau
Nieder-Moos
Nieder-Mörlen
Nieder-Mumbach
Nieder-Ofleiden
Nieder-Ohmen
Nieder-Olm
Nieder-Raidenbach
Nieder-Ramstadt
Nieder-Roden
Nieder-Rosbach

Nieder-Saulheim
Nieder-Seemen
Nieder-Steinheim
Nieder-Stoll
Nieder-Trausa
Nieder-Weinheim
Nieder-Weisel
Nieder-Widdersheim
Nieder-Wiesen
Nieder-Wöllstadt
Niederndorf
Niedernhausen
Niederwald
Nierstein
Nikolauspforte
Nonnen-Aue
Nonnen-Hof
Nonnenroth
Nonrod
Nordheim
Nösberts
Nösberts-Weidmoos
Nübel
Obbornhofen
Ober-Absteinach
Ober-Aue
Ober-Beerbach
Ober-Bessingen
Ober-Breidenbach
Ober-Dauernheim
Ober-Erlenbach
Ober-Eschbach
Ober-Finkenbach
Ober-Flörsheim
Ober-Florstadt
Ober-Gersprenz
Ober-Gleen
Ober-Grubenbach
Ober-Hainbrunn
Ober-Hambach
Ober-Hebstahl
Ober-Hilbersheim
Ober-Hiltersklingen
Ober-Hörgern
Ober-Ingelheim

Ober-Kainsbach
Ober-Kinzig
Ober-Kleingumpen
Ober-Klingen
Ober-Kreidach
Ober-Lais
Ober-Laudenbach
Ober-Liebersbach
Ober-Mengelbach
Ober-Mockstadt
Ober-Modau
Ober-Moos
Ober-Mörlen
Ober-Mossau
Ober-Mumbach
Ober-Nauses
Ober-Ofleiden
Ober-Ohmen
Ober-Olm
Ober-Ostern
Ober-Raidelbach
Ober-Ramstadt
Ober-Roden
Ober-Rohrbach
Ober-Rohrheim
Ober-Rosbach
Ober-Saulheim
Ober-Scharbach
Ober-Schmitten
Ober-Schönmattenwaag
Ober-Seemen
Ober-Seibertenrod
Ober-Sensbach
Ober-Sickendorf
Ober-Sorg
Ober-Steinberg
Ober-Steinheim
Ober-Traisa
Ober-Wegfurth
Ober-Widdersheim
Ober-Wöllstadt
Oberau
Oberaue
Oberburg
Oberbusch

Oberndorf
Obernhausen
Obernseener
Oberod
Oberrod
Oberseener Hof
Oberstraßheimer Hof
Obertshausen
Ockenheim
Ockstadt
Odenhausen
Odernheim
Oes
Offenbach am Main
Offenbach-Bieber
Offenheim
Offenthal
Offstein
Ofleiden
Ohmen
Ohmes
Ohrenbach
Olfen
Olfer Hof
Olm
Oppelshausen
Oppenheim
Oppenrod
Oppershofen
Oppertshausen
Orles
Orleshausen
Ortenberg
Ossenheim
Ostenburg
Ostern
Ostheim
Osthofen
Otterbach
Otzberg
Partenheim
Patershausen
Petersau
Petershainer Hof
Petterweil

Pfaffen-Beerfurth
Pfaffen-Schwabenheim
Pfaffenhof
Pfaffenhofen
Pfälzer Höfe
Pfalzhof
Pfalzraibach
Pfalzwiebelsbach
Pfeddersheim
Pfefferhöhe
Pferdsbach
Pfiffligheim
Pfirschbach
Pfordt
Pfungstadt
Philippseck
Philippseich
Philippshospital
Plackenhof
Planig
Plattenhof
Pleitersheim
Pohl
Pohl-Göns
Preußischer Hof
Quattelbach
Queck
Queckborn
Rabenau
Rabertshausen
Rad
Rad-Mühl
Radheim
Rai
Rai-Breitenbach
Raibach
Raidelbach
Rainrod
Ramstadt
Ranstadt
Rapsgrund
Raubach
Raubenstein
Rauchenau
Rauenthaler Hof

Rauna
Raunheim
Rebgeshain
Rebsgrund
Rechberg
Rehbach
Reibertenrod
Reichelsheim im Odenwald
Reichelsheim in der Wetterau
Reichenbach
Reichenberg
Reichlos
Reimenrod
Reimeroth
Reinhardshain
Reinhäuser
Reinheim
Reinrod
Reisen
Reisenkreuz
Reiskirchen
Remayer Hof
Rembrücken
Rendel
Renzendorf
Retschenhäuser Hof
Reuters
Rhein-Dürkheim
Rheinfelden
Richen
Richthof
Riedhäuser Hof
Riedrode
Rimbach
Rimborn
Rimhorn
Rimlos
Rinderbügen
Ringauer Hof
Ringelshausen
Ritterhof
Rittschlich
Rixfeld
Rochusberg
Rockenberg

Rodau
Rodau bei Bensheim
Rodau bei Lichtenberg
Roden
Rodenbach
Rodenstein
Rödgen
Rodheim
Rodheim an der Horloff
Rodheim vor der Höhe
Rodheimer Hof
Roggenwörth
Rohrbach
Rohrbach bei Reinheim
Rohrheim
Rohrs-Haus
Rombach
Rommelhausen
Rommersheim
Romrod
Ronneburg
Roosscher Hof
Roßbach
Rosbach
Roßdorf
Rosenbach
Rosengarten
Rosscher Hof
Rote Warte
Roter Kandel
Rothenberg
Röthges
Rückenaue
Rückerts-Hof
Rüddingshausen
Rudelsheim
Rudingshain
Rudlos
Ruhlkirchen
Rülfenrod
Rumpenheim
Ruppertenrod
Ruppertsburg
Rüsselsheim
Ruthardshausen

Ruttershausen
Saasen
Salinenhof
Salmshütte
Salz
Salzhausen
Salzungen
Sand-Hof
Sandaue
Sandbach
Sandbach-Uhlerborn
Sandhof
Sandlofs
Sandwoogbrücke
Sankt Johann
Sassen
Sauber
Sauber-Schwabenheim
Saubuche
Saulheim
Schaafheim
Schadenbach
Schadges
Schafhausen
Schafhof
Schannenbach
Schannenbacher Tal
Scharbach
Schardt-Hof
Scheibelhof
Schelln-Hof
Schellnhausen
Schiffenberg
Schimbach
Schimsheim
Schlechtenwegen
Schleiersbach
Schleifeld
Schlichter
Schlieglofs-Hof
Schlierbach
Schlitz
Schloß-Nauses
Schmal-Beerbach
Schmitt-Hof

Schmitten
Schmittshausen
Schneppenhausen
Schnorrenbach
Schöllenbach
Schönau
Schönberg
Schönbrunn
Schönhausen
Schönhof
Schönmattenwaag
Schönnen
Schornsheim
Schotten
Schusterwörth
Schützenrain
Schwabenheim
Schwabenrod
Schwabsburg
Schwalheim
Schwalheimer Hof
Schwanheim
Schwarz
Schwickartshausen
Seckmauern
See-Hof
Seeheim
Seehof
Seemen
Seibelsdorf
Seibertenrod
Seidenbach
Seidenbuch
Selgen-Hof
Seligenstadt
Sellnrod
Selters
Selzen
Semd
Sensbach
Sensfelder Hof
Sichenhausen
Sickendorf
Sickenhofen
Siedelsbrunn

Siefersheim
Siegmundshäuser Höfe
Silbergrube
Silgen-Hof
Sion
Södel
Solms
Solms-Ilsdorf
Sommerhof
Sommersgrund
Sonderbach
Sorg
Sorge
Sörgenloch
Spachbrücken
Spechtbach
Spiesheim
Spitzaltheim
Sponsheim
Sporkenheim
Sprendlingen
St. Johann
Stadecken
Staden
Staffel
Stallenkandel
Stammheim
Stangenrod
Staudenheimer Hof
Staufenberg
Steckelsberger Hof
Steigerts
Stein am Rhein
Stein-Bockenheim
Steinach
Steinacker
Steinau
Steinbach
Steinbach am Taunus
Steinberg
Steinbrückerteich
Steinbuch
Steinertswiese
Steines-Hof
Steinfurt

Steinfurth
Steinheim am Rhein
Steinkaut
Steinswörth
Stettbach
Stettbacher Tal
Stierbach
Stockau
Stockhausen
Stockhäuser Hof
Stockheim
Stockmannshof
Stockstadt
Stoll
Stollmühle
Storndorf
Stornfels
Straßheim
Strebendorf
Streitbach
Streithain
Stubenwald-Hof
Stumpertenrod
Sülzen
Sulzheim
Tal-Hof
Tal-Hof
Taschengrube
Tempelsee
Thiergarten
Thomashütte
Tiefenthal
Tiergarten
Tönges-Hof
Trais
Trais-Horloff
Trais-Münzenberg
Traisa bei Darmstadt
Traisa
Trautheim
Trebur
Treburer Hof
Treburer Oberwald
Treburer Unterwald
Treis an der Lumda

Trohe
Tromm
Trösel
Überau
Udenhausen
Udenheim
Uelversheim
Uffhofen
Uhlerborn
Ulfa
Üllershausen
Ulrichstein
Ulvenhöfe
Ülversheim
Umstadt
Undenheim
Unter-Absteinach
Unter-Breidenbach
Unter-Eichen
Unter-Finkenbach
Unter-Flockenbach
Unter-Florstadt
Unter-Gersprenz
Unter-Grubenbach
Unter-Hainbrunn
Unter-Hambach
Unter-Hammer
Unter-Hebstahl
Unter-Hiltersklingen
Unter-Kreidach
Unter-Lais
Unter-Liebersbach
Unter-Mengelbach
Unter-Mossau
Unter-Mumbach
Unter-Ostern
Unter-Raidelbach
Unter-Scharbach
Unter-Schmitten
Unter-Schönmattenwaag
Unter-Schwarz
Unter-Seibertenrod
Unter-Sensbach
Unter-Sickendorf
Unter-Sorg

Unter-Wegfurth
Unter-Widdersheim
Unterau
Unterdiebach
Uppershausen
Urberach
Usenborn
Utphe
Utschhausen
Ützhausen
Vadenrod
Vaitshain
Veitsberg
Vendersheim
Vielbrunn
Viernheim
Vietmes-Hof
Vilbel
Villingen
Vöckelsbach
Vöckelsberger Hof
Vockenrod
Vogelsberger Hof
Vohberg-Hof
Volkartshain
Volxheim
Vonhausen
Vorholz
Wächtersbach
Wackernheim
Wahlen
Wahlheim
Wahlheimer Hof
Wald
Wald-Amorbach
Wald-Bergheim
Wald-Bullau
Wald-Erlenbach
Wald-Hof
Wald-Holf
Wald-Michelbach
Wald-Uelversheim
Wäldershausen
Waldhaus
Waldhausen

Waldschützenhause
Wallbach
Walldorf
Wallenrod
Wallernhausen
Wallersdorf
Wallerstädten
Wallertheim
Wallhausen
Walsheim
Waltersbach
Wart-Hof
Waschenbach
Wasserbiblos
Wasserburg
Wasserloch
Wattenheim
Watzenborn
Watzenborn-Steinberg
Webern
Weckesheim
Wegfurth
Wehnerts
Wehrzollhaus
Weickartshain
Weid-Moos
Weidenhof
Weiher
Weiherhof
Weilerwald
Weinheim
Weinolsheim
Weinsheim
Weisel
Weisenau
Weißenstein
Weisheim
Weiskirchen
Weiten
Weiten-Gesäß
Weitershain
Weiterstadt
Weitzendorf
Weitzhain
Welgesheim

Wellershäuser Hof
Welzheim
Wembach
Wendelsheim
Wenings
Wernges
Wernings
Wersau
Weschnitz
Westerhaus
Westhofen
Westphälischer Hof
Wetterfeld
Wetterhof
Wettsaasen
Wetzkeil
Wickstadt
Widdersheim
Wiebelsbach
Wiedermus
Wies-Oppenheim
Wiesberger Hof
Wieseck
Wiesen
Wiesen-Hof
Wiesental
Wild-Hof
Wildbahn
Wildehirschhof
Wildhof
Willina
Willofs
Wilmshausen
Wimpfen
Windhain
Windhausen
Windhäuser
Windhof
Wingershausen
Winkel
Winnerod
Winterkasten
Winternheim
Wintersheim
Winterstein
Wippenbach
Wirberg
Wißberg

Wisselsheim
Wixhausen
Wohnbach
Wohnfeld
Wolf
Wolfer-Hof
Wölfersheim
Wolfsgarten
Wolfsheim
Wolfskehlen
Wolfslauf
Wöllstadt
Wöllstein
Wonsheim
Woogsdamm
Worfelden
Worms
Wörrstadt
Wörth
Wünschbach
Wünschen-Moos
Würzberg
Wurzelbach
Wüst
Wüst-Amorbach
Wüsten
Wüsten-Eddersheim
Ywen
Zahlbach
Zahmen
Zeilbach
Zeilhard
Zell
Zellhausen
Zeppelinheim
Ziegelhohl
Ziegelschal
Ziegenberg
Ziergiebelshof
Zimmern
Zipfen
Zornheim
Zotzenbach
Zotzenheim
Zuckerbuckel
Zwiefalten
Zwingenberg

Reverse Alphabetical Index of German Provinces

Below is a list comprising nearly 400 names of German provinces, i.e., kingdoms, duchies, principalities, and counties, such as *Baden, Coburg, Schleswig*. All political units from the county (*Grafschaft*) level up are listed. Those smaller (*Herrschaft*) are often inconsequential in size and importance and are thus not shown here. Included in this index are the names of districts, regions, and areas not defined by exact boundaries, such as *Propstei, Wetterau, Thüringer Wald*.

In historical records regional terms are often entitled "state" or "district" etc. and words of this type are also found in this list. Many political units had names consisting of two or more terms, such as *Sachsen-Coburg-Gotha* or *Hessen-Nassau*. Because such names were legion a few centuries ago, only the individual names are included herein.

Often the records of older documents in Germany describe a region in adverbial or prepositional terms, such as *[he was born] im Westfälischen* or *[he comes] aus dem Mainz'schen*. The suffix *-isch-* or *-sch-* should be removed before the term can be found in this list.

Extensive details on the political units listed here are found in the book *Historisches Lexikon der deutschen Länder* [Historical Encyclopedia of German Provinces] by Gerhard Köbler (Munich: Beck, 1990; FHL book no. 943 E3k 1990).

Fulda	Thüringerwald
Tenda	Arnsbergerwald
Gotha	Teutoburgerwald
Rossla	Bayrischerwald
Jena	Westerwald
Rheina	Pfälzerwald
Gera	Schwarzwald
Lohra	Saalfeld
Werra	Birkenfeld
Hoya	Biesterfeld
Schwäbisch Alb	Eichsfeld
Fränkisch Alb	Mansfeld
Wied	Hersfeld
Neuwied	Dänische Wohld
Manderscheid	Römhild
Reifferscheid	Detmold
Spreewald	Land
Odenwald	Bergisches Land
Mittenwald	Wendland
Steigerwald	Seeland

Ammeland	Brieg
Weserbergland	Wolfegg
Memelland	Königsegg
Havelland	Braunschweig
Samland	Schleswig
Ermland	Tittmoning
Rheinland	Jüterbog
Helgoland	Henneberg
Saarland	Kirchberg
Siegerland	Spiegelberg
Harlingerland	Stolberg
Münsterland	Württemberg
Sauerland	Neuwürttemberg
Friesland	Heiligenberg
Nordfriesland	Trachenberg
Ostfriesland	Hohenberg
Emsland	Kalenberg
Vogtland	Dannenberg
Naugard	Eisenberg
Elbe	Leuchtenberg
Stade	Wartenberg
Lüneburger Heide	Ortenberg
Wernigerode	Fürstenberg
Mangfalgebirge	Klettenberg
Fichtelgebirge	Wittenberg
Elbsandsteingebirge	Lauenberg
Rothaargebirge	Münzenberg
Schiefergebirge	Sternberg
Ammergebirge	Landsberg
Erzgebirge	Gudensberg
Osterzgebirge	Ravensberg
Nahe	Arnsberg
Reuss jüngere Linie	Rietberg
Reuss ältere Linie	Magdeburg
Brake	Bückeburg
Celle	Berleburg
Werle	Virneburg
Lippe	Lüneburg
Bergstrasse	Merseburg
Weinstrasse	Ratzeburg
Neisse	Trauchburg
Kleve	Weilburg
Deggendorf	Hamburg
Bonndorf	Limburg
Ebersdorf	Homburg

Naumburg	Bayreuth
Schaumburg	Probstei
Oldenburg	Lübeck
Brandenburg	Waldeck
Hardenburg	Rieneck
Aschaffenburg	Rostock
Toggenburg	Osnabrück
Rogenburg	Hunsrück
Hachenburg	Mark
Hohenburg	Nordmark
Blankenburg	Kurmark
Starkenburg	Altmark
Mecklenburg	Bezirk
Tecklenburg	Tal
Nellenburg	Thal
Altenburg	Philippsthal
Ortenburg	Eifel
Wittenburg	Kiel
Rottenburg	Runkel
Lauenburg	Holzappel
Neuenburg	Mosel
Coburg	Kassel
Harburg	Innviertel
Marburg	Wolfenbüttel
Sonderburg	Reckenheim
Augsburg	Blankenheim
Glücksburg	Pappenheim
Neuburg	Sponheim
Schwarzburg	Heitersheim
Würzburg	Bentheim
Ansbach	Krautheim
Mosbach	Salm
Sulzbach	Herzogthum
Butzbach	Herzogtum
Eisenach	Fürstentum
Urach	Sagan
Wurzach	Schwaben
Reich	Oberschwaben
Königreich	Baden
Kaiserreich	Winterrieden
Vorderösterreich	Schleiden
Jülich	Schmalkalden
Nörvenich	Wenden
Carolath	Minden
Barth	Verden

45

Saarwerden	Niedersachsen
Dresden	Posen
Grubenhagen	Hessen
Wredenhagen	Rhein-Hessen
Ellwangen	Ober-Hessen
Lingen	Kurhessen
Tübingen	Meissen
Kehdingen	Preussen
Stühlingen	Südpreussen
Wittislingen	Westpreussen
Leiningen	Ostpreussen
Meiningen	Burghausen
Veringen	Hildburghausen
Lothringen	Bruchhausen
Oberlothringen	Sondershausen
Rüstringen	Wursten
Thüringen	Wurzen
Usingen	Bautzen
Göttingen	Main
Katzenelnbogen	Ziegenhain
Rügen	Rhein
Kaichen	Nordrhein
Altenkirchen	Idstein
Partenkirchen	Königstein
Teschen	Holstein
Dithmarschen	Gerolstein
Norderdithmarschen	Wittgenstein
Süderdithmarschen	Frankenstein
Köthen	Ochsenstein
Schlesien	Hauenstein
Oberschlesien	Löwenstein
Niederschlesien	Hohnstein
Thüringer Becken	Eberstein
Zweibrücken	Berlin
Saarbrücken	Cammin
Franken	Schwerin
Mittelfranken	Stettin
Oberfranken	Hadeln
Unterfranken	Oppeln
Westfalen	Köln
Hundemen	Inn
Bremen	Nation
Alpen	Stormarn
Masuren	Hohenzollern
Sachsen	Simmern

Pommern	Elsass
Hinterpommern	Ober-Elsass
Vorpommern	Nieder-Elsass
Schlüchtern	Pless
Lautern	Reuss
Bevern	Taunus
Bayern	Staat
Rheinbayern	Dekanat
Oberbayern	Stadt
Niederbayern	Rudolstadt
Sayn	Darmstadt
Plön	Immenstadt
Stolp	Halberstadt
Neckar	Gebiet
Goslar	Grafschaft
Wetzlar	Herrschaft
Fritzlar	Anhalt
Hadamar	Amt
Weimar	Oberamt
Horstmar	Hallermunt
Isar	Rot
Trier	Spessart
Bischweiler	Pfirt
Ottweiler	Steinfurt
Weser	Querfurt
Münster	Delmenhorst
Wetter	Gau
Jauer	Lindau
Hannover	Sundgau
Speyer	Hegau
Ruhr	Hennegau
Ratibor	Chiemgau
Zator	Traungau
Kleves	Glogau
Kreis	Torgau
Landkreis	Breisgau
Stadtkreis	Klettgau
Oels	Grottkau
Werdenfels	Wohlau
Rothenfels	Breslau
Rheinfels	Lichtenau
Ems	Steinau
Solms	Weilnau
Hohensolms	Donau
Moers	Troppau

Wetterau	Oberpfalz
Nassau	Kurpfalz
Dessau	Veldenz
Sprottau	Mainz
Allgäu	Provinz
Jerichow	Rheinprovinz
Gützkow	Harz
Wustrow	Glatz
Güstrow	Metz
Valley	Zeitz
Schleiz	Strelitz
Greiz	Görlitz
Fränkische Schweiz	Schweidnitz
Märkische Schweiz	Liegnitz
Holsteinische Schweiz	Lausitz
Sächsische Schweiz	Oberlausitz
Pfalz	Niederlausitz
Rheinpfalz	Auschwitz

An old mill in Erbach

Alphabetical Index of German Provinces

Allgäu
Alpen
Altenburg
Altenkirchen
Altmark
Ammeland
Ammergebirge
Amt
Anhalt
Ansbach
Arnsberg
Arnsbergerwald
Aschaffenburg
Augsburg
Auschwitz
Baden
Barth
Bautzen
Bayern
Bayreuth
Bayrischerwald
Bentheim
Bergisches Land
Bergstrasse
Berleburg
Berlin
Bevern
Bezirk
Biesterfeld
Birkenfeld
Bischweiler
Blankenburg
Blankenheim
Bonndorf
Brake
Brandenburg
Braunschweig
Breisgau
Bremen
Breslau
Brieg
Bruchhausen

Bückeburg
Burghausen
Butzbach
Cammin
Carolath
Celle
Chiemgau
Coburg
Dänische Wohld
Dannenberg
Darmstadt
Deggendorf
Dekanat
Delmenhorst
Dessau
Detmold
Dithmarschen
Donau
Dresden
Ebersdorf
Eberstein
Eichsfeld
Eifel
Eisenach
Eisenberg
Elbe
Elbsandsteingebirge
Ellwangen
Elsass
Ems
Emsland
Ermland
Erzgebirge
Falkenburg
Fichtelgebirge
Franken
Frankenstein
Fränkisch Alb
Fränkische Schweiz
Friesland
Fritzlar
Fulda

Fürstenberg
Fürstentum
Gau
Gebiet
Gera
Gerolstein
Glatz
Glogau
Glücksburg
Görlitz
Goslar
Gotha
Gotha
Göttingen
Grafschaft
Greiz
Grottkau
Grubenhagen
Gudensberg
Güstrow
Gützkow
Hachenburg
Hadamar
Hadeln
Halberstadt
Hallermunt
Hamburg
Hannover
Harburg
Hardenburg
Harlingerland
Harz
Hauenstein
Havelland
Hegau
Heiligenberg
Heitersheim
Helgoland
Henneberg
Hennegau
Herrschaft
Hersfeld
Herzogthum
Herzogtum
Hessen

Hildburghausen
Hinterpommern
Hohenberg
Hohenburg
Hohensolms
Hohenzollern
Hohnstein
Holstein
Holsteinische Schweiz
Holzappel
Homburg
Horstmar
Hoya
Hundemen
Hunsrück
Idstein
Immenstadt
Inn
Innviertel
Isar
Istein
Jauer
Jena
Jerichow
Jülich
Jülich-Kleves
Jüterbog
Kaichen
Kaiserreich
Kalenberg
Kassel
Katzenelnbogen
Kehdingen
Kiel
Kirchberg
Klettenberg
Klettgau
Kleve
Köln
Königreich
Königsegg
Königstein
Köthen
Krautheim
Kreis

Kurhessen
Kurmark
Kurpfalz
Land
Landkreis
Landsberg
Lauenberg
Lauenburg
Lausitz
Lautern
Leiningen
Leuchtenberg
Lichtenau
Liegnitz
Limburg
Lindau
Lingen
Lippe
Lohra
Lothringen
Löwenstein
Lübeck
Lüneburg
Lüneburger Heide
Magdeburg
Main
Mainz
Manderscheid
Mangfalgebirge
Mansfeld
Marburg
Mark
Märkische Schweiz
Masuren
Mecklenburg
Meiningen
Meissen
Memelland
Merseburg
Metz
Minden
Mittelfranken
Mittenwald
Moers
Mosbach

Mosel
Münster
Münsterland
Münzenberg
Nahe
Nassau
Nation
Naugard
Naumburg
Neckar
Neisse
Nellenburg
Neuburg
Neuenburg
Neuwied
Neuwürttemberg
Niederbayern
Nieder-Elsass
Niederlausitz
Niedersachsen
Niederschlesien
Norderdithmarschen
Nordfriesland
Nordmark
Nordrhein
Nörvenich
Oberamt
Oberbayern
Ober-Elsass
Oberfranken
Ober-Hessen
Oberlausitz
Oberlothringen
Oberpfalz
Oberschlesien
Oberschwaben
Ochsenstein
Odenwald
Oels
Oldenburg
Oppeln
Ortenberg
Ortenburg
Osnabrück
Osterzgebirge

Ostfriesland
Ostpreussen
Ottweiler
Pappenheim
Partenkirchen
Pfalz
Pfälzerwald
Pfirt
Philippsthal
Pless
Plön
Pommern
Posen
Preussen
Probstei
Provinz
Querfurt
Ratibor
Ratzeburg
Ravensberg
Reckenheim
Reich
Reifferscheid
Reuss
Reuss ältere Linie
Reuss jüngere Linie
Rhein
Rhein-Hessen
Rheina-Wolbeck
Rheinbayern
Rheinfels
Rheinland
Rheinland-Pfalz
Rheinpfalz
Rheinprovinz
Rieneck
Rietberg
Rogenburg
Römhild
Rossla
Rostock
Rot
Rothaargebirge
Rothenfels
Rottenburg

Rudolstadt
Rügen
Ruhr
Runkel
Rüstringen
Saalfeld
Saarbrücken
Saarland
Saarwerden
Sachsen
Sächsische Schweiz
Sagan
Salm
Samland
Sauerland
Sayn
Schaumburg
Schiefergebirge
Schleiden
Schleiz
Schlesien
Schleswig
Schlüchtern
Schmalkalden
Schwaben
Schwäbisch Alb
Schwarzburg
Schwarzwald
Schweidnitz
Schwerin
Seeland
Siegerland
Simmern
Solms
Sonderburg
Sondershausen
Spessart
Speyer
Spiegelberg
Sponheim
Spreewald
Sprottau
Staat
Stade
Stadt

Stadtkreis
Starkenburg
Steigerwald
Steinau
Steinfurt
Sternberg
Stettin
Stolberg
Stolp
Stormarn
Strelitz
Stühlingen
Süderdithmarschen
Südpreussen
Sulzbach
Sundgau
Tal
Taunus
Tecklenburg
Tenda
Teschen
Teutoburgerwald
Thal
Thüringen
Thüringer Becken
Thüringerwald
Tittmoning
Toggenburg
Torgau
Trachenberg
Trauchburg
Traungau
Trier
Troppau
Tübingen
Unterfranken
Urach
Usingen
Valley
Veldenz
Verden
Veringen
Virneburg
Vogtland
Vorderösterreich

Vorpommern
Waldeck
Wartenberg
Weilburg
Weilnau
Weimar
Weinstrasse
Wenden
Wendland
Werdenfels
Werle
Wernigerode
Werra
Weser
Weserbergland
Westerwald
Westfalen
Westpreussen
Wetter
Wetterau
Wetzlar
Wied
Winterrieden
Wittenberg
Wittenburg
Wittgenstein
Wittislingen
Wohlau
Wolfegg
Wolfenbüttel
Wredenhagen
Wursten
Württemberg
Wurzach
Würzburg
Wurzen
Wustrow
Zator
Zeitz
Ziegenhain
Zweibrücken

Spelling Variations in German Names:
Solving Family History Research Problems
Through Applications of German and English Phonetics
by Roger P. Minert, Ph.D.,A.G.

Contents:

Short history of German spelling conventions and grammar
Basic phonetic theories about how vowels and consonants are formed in the mouth
Descriptions of the ways in which specific vowels and consonants are exchanged
Examples of vowel and consonant variations among German dialect regions
Examples of vowel and consonant variations between Europe and North America

Special Features:

Sample names to show evidence of each phonetic variation described
Illustrations culled from genuine vital records to show the principles in practice
Checklists of tactics for identifying variant spellings in Europe and North America.
Trouble-shooting guide to spelling variations of over 200 surnames and place names

Enthusiastically endorsed by renowned genealogists **Trudy Schenk** and **Horst Reschke**.

Filling a crucial gap in the self-help literature on German family history research!

* *

Hesse Place Name Indexes:
Identifying Place Names Using Alphabetical and Reverse Alphabetical Indexes
and
Palatine Place Name Indexes:
Identifying Place Names Using Alphabetical and Reverse Alphabetical Indexes
by Roger P. Minert, Ph.D., A.G.

How these index collections will save you time and effort in genealogical research:
The *Alphabetical Indexes* will help you to...

...determine whether the town in question was in Hesse/the Bavarian Palatinate
...check the spelling of extracted names for correctness
...produce an entire place name from an abbreviation
...complete a place name for which the last letters are missing.

The *Reverse Alphabetical Indexes* will help you to...

...complete a place name for which the first letter(s) is/are missing due to torn or rotted
pages, difficult handwriting, poor photocopying or microfilming, etc.
...check the spelling of extracted names for correctness
...avoid checking out potentially hundreds of names in gazetteers to discover which
name(s) might end with the few letters that are identifiable.

Bonus features of these two books:

Description of tactics for identifying and deciphering place names
Alphabetical index of names of German provinces and geographical regions
Reverse alphabetical index of names of German provinces and geographical regions

The only reverse alphabetical indexes available outside of the Family History Library!

ORDER FORM: *GRT Publications*

To order these books, simply fill out this page, enclose your payment, and send them to the address below.

Title: *Spelling Variations in German Names*

©2000 GRT Publications   8.5 X 11   92 pp., softb.   ISBN 0-9678420-1-8

Price per copy (includes shipping and handling): $ 17.75

Utah residents please add sales tax (6.25% = $1.11):   _____

Total for *Spelling* $_____

Postage Outside of North America/Europe add $3 (surface) or $7 (air) for EACH book ordered: _____

Title: *Hesse Place Name Indexes*

©2000 GRT Publications   8.5 X 11   62 pp., softb.   ISBN 0-9678420-0-X

Price per copy (includes shipping and handling): $ 11.95

Utah residents please add sales tax (6.25% = $0.75):   _____

Total for *Hesse* $_____

Postage Outside of North America/Europe add $2 (surface) or $5 (air) for EACH book ordered: _____

Title: *Palatine Place Name Indexes*

©2000 GRT Publications   8.5 X 11   60 pp., softb.   ISBN 0-9678420-2-6

Price per copy (includes shipping and handling): $ 11.95

Utah residents please add sales tax (6.25% = $0.75):   _____

Total for *Palatine* $_____

Postage Outside of North America/Europe add $2 (surface) or $5 (air) for EACH book ordered: _____

Grand Total U.S. $_____

* *

Please make your check or money order payable to *GRT Publications*. Sorry, we cannot accept credit cards. Please do not send cash.

Send order form and check or   The book(s) will be shipped to:
money order to:

                                                 Name:_____

GRT Publications
1001 S. 1020 West   Address:_____
Woods Cross, UT
84087-2074   USA   City, State/Zip:_____

In Europa: Zur Bestellung des Buches *Spelling*... überweisen Sie bitte DM 39,- bzw. Euro 19,- pro Exemplar auf das u.a. Konto. Bitte geben Sie unbedingt das Stichwort *Spelling* und Ihre genaue Anschrift auf dem Überweisungsformular an, damit Ihnen das Buch umgehend zugesandt werden kann.

Zur Bestellung des Buches *Hesse*... bzw. *Palatine*... überweisen Sie bitte DM 27,- bzw. Euro 14,- pro Exemplar auf das u.a. Konto mit dem Stichwort *Hesse..* bzw. *Palatine*....

                Konto-Nr. 37 211 013 Roger P. Minert
                Stadtsparkasse Hannover BLZ 250 501 80